Bryan Doerries

ALL THAT YOU'VE SEEN HERE IS GOD
NEW VERSIONS OF FOUR GREEK TRAGEDIES

Bryan Doerries is a writer, director, and translator. He is the founder of Theater of War, a project that presents readings of ancient Greek plays to service members, veterans, caregivers, and families to help them initiate conversations about the visible and invisible wounds of war. He is also the cofounder of Outside the Wire, a social impact company that uses theater and a variety of other media to address pressing public health and social issues, such as combat-related psychological injury, end-of-life care, prison reform, domestic violence, political violence, recovery from natural and man-made disasters, substance abuse, and addiction. A self-described evangelist for classical literature and its relevance to our lives today, Doerries uses age-old approaches to help individuals and communities heal from suffering and loss.

For more information about his work, please visit:
www.outsidethewirellc.com.

ALSO BY BRYAN DOERRIES

The Theater of War: What Ancient Greek Tragedies
Can Teach Us Today

ALL THAT YOU'VE
SEEN HERE IS GOD

ALL THAT YOU'VE SEEN HERE IS GOD

New Versions of Four Greek Tragedies

Sophocles' *Ajax*, *Philoctetes*, and *Women of Trachis*
& Aeschylus' *Prometheus Bound*

Bryan Doerries

VINTAGE BOOKS
A DIVISION OF PENGUIN RANDOM HOUSE LLC
NEW YORK

FIRST VINTAGE BOOKS EDITION, SEPTEMBER 2015

Copyright © 2015 by Bryan Doerries

All rights reserved. Published in the United States by Vintage Books, a division of Penguin Random House LLC, New York, and distributed in Canada by Random House of Canada, a division of Penguin Random House Ltd., Toronto.

Vintage and colophon are registered trademarks of Penguin Random House LLC.

Philoctetes was originally published by Vintage Books, a division of Penguin Random House LLC, New York, in 2014.

The Library of Congress Cataloging-in-Publication Data
All that you've seen here is God : new versions of four Greek tragedies : Ajax, Philoctetes, and Women of Trachis by Sophocles & Prometheus bound by Aeschylus / translated by Bryan Doerries.
pages   cm
1. Greek drama—Translations into English. I. Doerries, Bryan.
II. Sophocles. Ajax. English. 2015. III. Sophocles. Philoctetes.
English. 2015. IV. Sophocles. Trachiniae. English. 2015.
V. Aeschylus. Prometheus bound. English. 2015.
PA3626.A2D65 2015   882'.01—dc23   2015010190

Vintage Books Trade Paperback ISBN: 978-0-307-94973-8
eBook ISBN: 978-0-307-94977-6

Book design by Claudia Martinez

www.vintagebooks.com

Printed in the United States of America
10 9 8 7 6 5 4 3 2

My friends,
you have seen
many strange things:
countless deaths,
new kinds of torture,
immeasurable pain,
and all that you've
seen here is god.
   —SOPHOCLES, *Women of Trachis*

CONTENTS

THE AUDIENCE AS TRANSLATOR

People who have lived lives of mythological proportions have no trouble relating to ancient Greek tragedies. Those who have been visited by disaster, who have survived trauma or witnessed death, those who have loved and grieved with equal intensity, or who know the meaning of sacrifice all possess an intuitive understanding of these ancient stories that no amount of study can acquire.

The ancient playwright Aeschylus wrote in his *Agamemnon* that we "learn through suffering." I would hasten to add that those who have suffered are uniquely able to teach us about ancient Greek tragedies and what they signify today. When people who know tragedy firsthand see their own private struggles reflected in stories that are thousands of years old, something is unlocked and revealed.

I first saw it happen in a cavernous hotel ballroom in San Diego with harsh white lighting and worn wall-to-wall carpeting, where nearly four hundred Marines and their spouses convened one summer night to hear scenes from Sophocles' *Ajax* and *Philoctetes* performed by seasoned New York actors, followed by a town hall discussion about the invisible wounds of war. Though I had translated the tragedies from the ancient Greek, and had a powerful hunch they would speak to combat veterans, I soon learned that these ancient war plays were written in a code that I needed military audiences to translate for me.

One of the first people to speak after the readings was a striking woman with weary blue eyes and an unassuming voice. "Hello. My name is Marshele Waddell," she said, "I am the proud mother of a Marine and the wife of a Navy SEAL. My husband went away four times to war and—just like Ajax—he came back dragging invisible bodies into our house. The war came home with him. And to quote from the play, 'Our home is a slaughterhouse.'"

A heavy silence hung over the room. Then, one after the other, the Marines and their loved ones stood up—a chaplain, a sergeant major, a general's wife, a wounded veteran, a psychiatrist, a colonel, a lance corporal—and testified to the truth of Sophocles' tragedies, quoting lines from memory and weaving them into their personal stories, as if they had known the ancient plays their entire lives. Though many of the Marines had never heard of the plays, let alone of Sophocles, few of them were strangers to the stories: the story of a highly decorated warrior who, after losing his friend in battle and being betrayed by his command, slides into a depression, goes on a killing spree, and takes his own life in shame; or the story of a combat veteran who is abandoned by his friends and his nation on a deserted island for nine long years after contracting a horrifying and debilitating chronic illness.

Sophocles' ability to speak to veterans and their families nearly twenty-five hundred years after his plays were first performed is no coincidence. It is well established that he served as a general in the Athenian army during a century in which Athens saw nearly eighty years of war. His plays were originally performed for an audience of some seventeen thousand citizen-soldiers. To be a citizen at that time meant being a soldier. Even the actors were likely to have been combat veterans. Many of the hard-won insights of ancient Greek tragedy were forged in the crucible of war. And so it follows that many of these ancient plays depict experiences that only those who've been to war, or cared for those who'd been to war, could possibly understand.*

Tragedy is an ancient military technology, a form of storytelling that evokes powerful emotions in order to erode stigmas, elicit empathy, generate dialogue, and stir citizens to action. When you plug a tragedy into a community that is ready to receive it, the story does what it was designed to do. Like the ancient Athenian audience in the Theater of Dionysus, the war-hardened Marines who gathered in the ballroom that night in San Diego knew the plays, not as representations of war and its aftermath, but as lived experience. They recognized and understood the characters and their conflicts. The stories spoke directly to them and their spouses, across millennia.

Over the last six years, I have directed readings of my translations of tragedies by Sophocles, Aeschylus, Euripides, and other ancient authors in places as wide ranging as the Pentagon, supermax prisons, homeless shelters, drug-ravaged Appalachian towns, churches, military bases, the Mayo Clinic, museums, regional theaters, business schools, children's hospitals, public squares, and the detention camps in Guantánamo Bay, Cuba, for audiences composed of combat veterans, first responders, hospice nurses, addicts, chronically and terminally ill patients, caregivers, students, spouses, prison guards, social workers, mental-health providers, doctors, chaplains, activists, and concerned citizens.

---

* The connection between tragedy and military service in fifth-century Athens has been made most forcefully and persuasively by the psychiatrist and author Jonathan Shay in "The Birth of Tragedy—Out of the Needs of Democracy," *Didaskalia: The Journal for Ancient Performance* 2, no. 2 (April 1995).

In listening to these audiences, in hearing their stories, I have discovered that I am, in fact, not the sole translator of the plays within these pages. I have learned from these audiences the true meaning of tragedy, and it is to them that I dedicate the following four plays.

TRANSLATOR'S NOTE

I begin all of my translations of ancient Greek tragedies with the original texts. However, what I am aiming for is not an alchemical—one-for-one—transmutation of ancient Greek into English, especially when it comes to idiom and meter. Obviously, that would be impossible and, likely, unspeakable. My goal is to build a bridge between the ancient and contemporary worlds, which inspires the reader, actor, and audience members to connect with the impulses beneath the original words, so that they might be swept up into the unfolding emergency that propels each play forward. My translations railroad, unimpeded, toward their conclusions in tight, tense columns and short bursts of text, not in an approximation of ancient Greek prosody, but rather a visual representation of how the words appear when filtered through my synapses. Finally, my translations are, by design, spare and incomplete. I am interested in how omission creates an opportunity for the reader or performer to imbue the space between words with meaning. I strive to provide readers with a foothold in the ancient original, while simultaneously inviting them to complete the translation by exploring the urgent need for the words to be spoken now.

SOPHOCLES' *AJAX*

AN INTRODUCTION

Sophocles' *Ajax* barrels toward disaster with the relentlessness of a crisis, leaving no time for the characters—or audience members, for that matter—to catch their breath. "Watching the play," remarked a veterans' court judge in East Lansing, Michigan, "was like looking on helplessly as a plane fell out of the sky and crashed at our feet." It would be hard to find a more fitting metaphor for this ancient tragedy. *Ajax,* after all, depicts the abrupt and precipitous mental disintegration of the strongest Greek warrior during the final year of the Trojan War.

The mighty Ajax was known as the "shield," because he and his soldiers shielded the Greeks from the worst of attacks, laying their lives on the front lines, sustaining the greatest losses. Ajax lived by a strict code, embodying the ancient warrior ethos. Second only to his cousin Achilles, he placed core values like honor, excellence, courage, and commitment above all others, and always tried to do the right thing, even in the fog of war.

When Achilles died, no one took the news of his loss harder than Ajax. By some accounts, Ajax was the warrior who carried the body of his fallen cousin and close friend over his shoulder off the battlefield. In the days that followed, Ajax naturally expected to receive Achilles' armor—one of the highest combat honors in the Trojan War, as well as a time-honored ritual of mourning. But the generals Agamemnon and Menelaus decided to hold funeral games to help boost troop morale, and planned to award Achilles' armor to the overall winner. One of the contests was speechmaking, and while Ajax was physically superior to all of his fellow soldiers, he was never great with words. He tried to make a speech, but instead he embarrassed himself in front of the Greek army.

Sulking on the sidelines, Ajax looked on helplessly as Odysseus—the director of Greek intelligence, who never laid his life on the line for anyone—swayed the crowd with a beautiful speech about why he, above all others, deserved the armor of Achilles.* At the end of the funeral games, when the judges announced their final decision, Ajax watched in disbelief as the generals awarded his close friend's armor to Odysseus, on the merits of his words rather than his deeds.

For Ajax, this decision was a betrayal of the highest order. It robbed him of his sense of honor, his identity, and—most important—his ability to grieve. And it was this toxic combination of betrayal, exhaustion, and displaced grief that finally pushed him over the edge. Stripped of his humanity, Ajax became a killing machine, no longer able to distinguish friend from foe, civilian from combatant, animal from human. He killed everything in sight, everything that breathed.

In a *New York Times* article entitled "Across America, Deadly Echoes of Foreign Battles," published on January 13, 2008,

---

* The description of the speechmaking contest and Odysseus' rhetorical victory over Ajax is not recounted in Sophocles' text. However, scholars conjecture that in Aeschylus' lost version of the story—*Hoplon Krisis*—Ajax and Odysseus vie for the armor of Achilles by making speeches about their respective merits. The extant fragments of the ancient Greek philosopher Antisthenes describe a similar battle of wits between the two warriors. Ovid's *Metamorphoses: Book XIII* also depicts the debate. Inspired by these accounts, I developed and fleshed out the details surrounding the speechmaking contest in my introductory remarks in order to heighten the stakes of the opening scene for actors, readers, and audiences.

as part of a series about the difficulties faced by returning veterans, the investigative reporters Deborah Sontag and Lizette Alvarez depicted how the violence from the wars in Iraq and Afghanistan had returned to American soil.* The article contained a summation of news headlines from across America:

> Town by town across the country, headlines have been telling similar stories. Lakewood, Wash.: "Family Blames Iraq After Son Kills Wife." Pierre, S.D.: "Soldier Charged With Murder Testifies About Postwar Stress." Colorado Springs: "Iraq War Vets Suspected in Two Slayings, Crime Ring."

Sontag and Alvarez reported that the *New York Times* had verified "121 cases in which veterans of Iraq and Afghanistan committed a killing in this country, or were charged with one, after their return from war." Of those cases, three-quarters involved service members who were still serving in the military when the murders took place.

> More than half the killings involved guns, and the rest were stabbings, beatings, strangulations and bathtub drownings. Twenty-five offenders faced murder, manslaughter or homicide charges for fatal car crashes resulting from drunken, reckless or suicidal driving. About a third of the victims were spouses, girlfriends, children or other relatives.

On every page of the article, in every paragraph, was written the story of Ajax.

---

* Sontag, D. and L. Alvarez, "Across America, Deadly Echoes of Foreign Battles." *New York Times,* January 13, 2008.

A quarter of the victims were fellow service members, including Specialist Richard Davis of the Army, who was stabbed repeatedly and then set ablaze, his body hidden in the woods by fellow soldiers a day after they all returned from Iraq.

From Sophocles' searing portrait of Ajax—a warrior struggling with the invisible wounds of war—it seems clear that psychological injury, what is now called PTSD, was a persistent issue for warriors twenty-five hundred years ago. Like Americans today, ancient Greek soldiers must have experienced the violence of war on and off the battlefield. In Afghanistan, the United States waged war for more than a decade, the longest war in its history. Uncannily, Sophocles' *Ajax* takes place in the final months of the Trojan War, when many of the greatest Greek warriors unraveled, snapped, and died after nearly a decade of nonstop fighting. Never before has the United States sent an all-volunteer force on this many deployments, and never before have so many combat veterans returned to a country in which so few Americans have been touched by the war in any meaningful way.

On March 11, 2012, an Army staff sergeant and trained sniper named Robert Bales, a decorated combat veteran on his fourth deployment in nine years, left his base in southern Afghanistan under cover of night, walked into a local village, and went door-to-door, shooting and stabbing Afghan civilians—many of them women and children. He then returned to base and, matter-of-factly, told a friend about what he had done, before walking into another village and slaughtering more civilians. Finally, he walked back to base at dawn, soaked in blood, and reportedly said to fellow soldiers that he thought he'd done "the right thing."

All told, Bales killed sixteen civilians in two separate attacks, setting many of their bodies ablaze, as boys and girls cowered behind curtains begging for mercy, screaming, "We are children! We are children!" In one harrowing detail, a young survivor—a fourteen-year-old boy—saw Bales enter his family's shed and open fire on their cow. Bales had a clean record, with no prior incidents or signs of mental-health issues. There are many theories as to why he snapped and what combination of factors—traumatic brain injury, post-traumatic stress, alcohol abuse, multiple deployments, steroid use, marital trouble, et cetera—transformed this seemingly normal soldier into an indiscriminate killing machine. Like Sophocles' *Ajax,* the story of Staff Sergeant Bales asks more questions than it will ever answer, but at the core of both stories—spanning thousands of years—remains one haunting question: At what cost?

CHARACTERS

(in order of appearance)

ODYSSEUS: *the director of Greek intelligence*

AJAX: *a formidable warrior*

ATHENA: *the goddess of war*

CHORUS: *the sailors and soldiers of Ajax*

TECMESSA: *the battle-won wife of Ajax*

EURYSACES: *their three-year-old son*

MESSENGER: *a soldier of the Greek army*

TEUCER: *the half brother of Ajax*

MENELAUS: *the deputy commander of the Greek army*

AGAMEMNON: *the commander of the Greek army*

ODYSSEUS *appears at dawn—low to the*
ground—darting in and out of shadows. He is
searching for a safe place to wait for AJAX.

ATHENA *startles him, a voice at the borders of*
darkness.

ATHENA

> Why am
> I never
> surprised,
> son of Laertes,
> to catch you
> stalking
> an enemy
> at daybreak,
> like a blood-
> hound after
> some scent,
> tracking foot-
> prints behind
> the tents
> where Ajax
> and his men
> hold down
> the battle line?

> You wish
> to know if
> he's inside,

soaked
in sweat
from the
slaughter?

Then tell me
what you've
come to do,
and you may
learn from one
who knows.

ODYSSEUS

Dearest Athena,
guardian goddess,
though your shape
evades my eyes,
I hear you clearly
in my mind, like
the tune of a song
to which I somehow
know the words.

I'm circling
in on an enemy,
just as you've guessed,
close on his heels.

I have come
for Ajax,
the one
we called
the "shield."

It is he alone whom I now hunt.

Last night,
he did some-

thing vile,
some vile
thing, some-
thing un-
imaginable,
if he is the one,
we cannot be sure,
still shaken by
the sight of it,
and so they
sent me here to
confirm what
he has done.

All of our cattle
are dead, and
the men who
tended them,
hacked to pieces,
butchered by
a hand—his,
we think—for
one of our men
swears to have
seen him sprinting
across the field
with a wet sword.

As soon as I heard,
I was on the case,
following the tracks,
which led me here,
but I've been thrown
by strange markings
in the mud and cannot
find him anywhere.

You have
arrived,
as always,
at the right
moment
to guide
me with
your hand.

ATHENA *steps out of the shadows.*

ATHENA

Obviously, Odysseus, I came to help with the
hunt.

ODYSSEUS

Then I am on the right track?

ATHENA

He is the one you describe: the killer of cows.

ODYSSEUS

A reckless gesture, but why did he do it?

ATHENA

Black bile—blinding rage—over the arms of
Achilles.

ODYSSEUS

But what drove him to attack the animals?

ATHENA

In his mind, their blood was yours.

ODYSSEUS

He wished to kill the Greeks?

ATHENA

Affirmative.

He would have completed his mission
had I not been paying attention.

ODYSSEUS

Where did he find the courage to do it?

ATHENA

He stalked you quietly in the night.

ODYSSEUS

How close did he come to his target?

ATHENA

Close enough to strike the generals.

ODYSSEUS

And what contained his bloodlust?

ATHENA

I did.

I robbed him
of the pleasure
of cutting you
to pieces,
raining on
his death
parade,
distracting
him with

visions of
bovine foes
grazing in
the fields
under
the watchful
eyes of simple
herdsmen.

He descended
upon them
with full fury,
ripping out horns
with his hands,
slitting throats
and snapping
spines, at one
point squeezing
the life from
a general, then
taking the lives
of other officers,
or so he thought,
trembling from
contamination.

I stoked his rage,
driving him deeper
into the snare.

Finally tired from
all the killing,
he bound and
gagged his sad
prisoners, those
pitiful few cows

and sheep some-
how still standing,
and rounded them
up for the death
march back to his
camp, convinced
they were men.

He tortures them inside the tent.

And now I will
expose you
to his illness,
so you may see
it with your
own eyes.

Stand there,
like a man.
He won't
hurt you,
as long as
I am here.

Don't worry.
I will hide you
in his blind spot;
he won't see you
in the shadows.

ATHENA *turns and shouts toward the tent.*

You, there,
in the tent,
stretching
prisoners
on the rack,
put down

your ropes;
report to me
immediately!

ODYSSEUS

What are you doing? Lower your voice.

ATHENA

Watch what you say. Someone might call you a
coward.

ODYSSEUS

Please, Athena, by the gods, let him stay inside the
tent.

ATHENA

He's only a man, not to be feared, the same as before.

ODYSSEUS

He was and is my enemy.

ATHENA

Well, isn't it satisfying to laugh at an enemy?

ODYSSEUS

It would please me more if he stayed within.

ATHENA

Are you afraid to gaze upon a maniac?

ODYSSEUS

When he was sane, I would have met his stare.

ATHENA

He won't see you standing before him.

ODYSSEUS

Isn't he looking through the same eyes?

ATHENA

I'll shade his eyes and darken his vision.

ODYSSEUS

Whatever the goddess wants, she takes.

ATHENA

Stand there silently. Do not move!

ODYSSEUS

I must remain, against my wishes.

ATHENA

AJAX!
I call you for a second time.
Please don't make it a third.
(I thought we were friends.)

AJAX *steps out of the shadows, covered in blood,*

AJAX

Athena,
daughter
of Zeus,
who stood
beside me
as I worked
last night,
I will not

soon forget
your loyalty,
and will honor
you with gold.

ATHENA

A lovely offer.
Thank you, sir.
Now tell me how
you smeared your
sword, plunging it
deep into the men
you came to hate.

AJAX

I hate to brag,
but the rights
are mine.

ATHENA

And did your weapon touch sons of Atreus?

AJAX

They will never disgrace my name again.

ATHENA

Then they are dead, if I understand you?

AJAX

Let's see them steal my arms now!

ATHENA

And what about the son of Laertes?
How did things turn out for him?
Or did he somehow get away?

AJAX

> Are you talking about the fox?

ATHENA

> Yes, your opponent, Odysseus.

AJAX

> Oh, he's a special case.
> He sits inside, shaking.
> I'm not yet ready to give
> him the pleasure of dying.

ATHENA

> What do you plan to do to him?

AJAX

> First, I will tie him to a stake.

ATHENA

> Then, what next?

AJAX

> I'll lash his back until it's red with blood.

ATHENA

> He's already suffered enough.
> Please don't torture this man.

AJAX (*with inappropriate force*)

> When it comes to anything else,
> Athena, I'll always obey your orders.
> But he will get what he deserves!

> > ATHENA's *face slackens. Her tone shifts.*

ATHENA

> If that's what you want,
> then do as you wish;
> spare no pleasure
> in this man's pain.

AJAX

> I . . . well . . .
> I'd better get
> back to work.

> I ask you to always
> stay on my side,
> just as you
> did last night.

> AJAX *dashes inside his tent.*
> ATHENA *faces* ODYSSEUS.

ATHENA

> Now you see
> the power
> of the gods.
> What man
> in memory
> was more careful
> always to do
> the right thing?

ODYSSEUS

> None I can recall.

> I feel sorry for him,
> though he hates me.

> A savage infection
> confuses his mind.

It could easily have been me.

I see now that
we are nothing
but shades
stumbling around
in the shadows.

ATHENA

Then take a good, long look
and never say an arrogant
word against the gods again,
or stick out your chest
because of your strength
or your abundant wealth.

In just one day, all things
living can be lifted up,
then buried deep below.

The gods always favor
those who stay on the path.

ATHENA *vanishes.*

But those who stray, they hate.

ODYSSEUS *sprints away.*
The CHORUS *appears on either side of the camp,*
debating desertion.

CHORUS

You noble son
of Telamon
from Salamis,
unsinkable,
though battered

on all sides by
mighty waves,
when Fortune
smiles on you
it brings me joy,
but when lightning
strikes above your
head, or Rumor
spreads from
camp to camp,
infecting the Greeks
with evil intentions,
I shiver to think
what will happen
to us all when
you are no longer
among the living.

Just before night
dissolved into day
I shot out of bed
to a deafening cry
full of slanderous
words claiming
you crept into
the fields where
the soldiers keep
their war spoils,
grazing on grass
and . . . Rumor has
it you slaughtered
these animals,
sliced them into
slabs of bleeding

meat with your
bright blade.

Words like these
travel quickly
around the camps
when whispered—
ear to ear—
with conviction by
men like Odysseus,
for what he says
rings true with
what we know
of your nature,
and those who
hear the story
relish every detail,
taking pleasure
in your troubles,
cursing your name.

Great men make easy targets.
Envy stalks them in the night.

Small men stand defenseless,
without leaders to protect them.

Great men need small men
to stand before them like a wall.

The generals will
never understand.

They are calling
for blood, and we
lack the strength
to fight them
off without you.

As soon as
you turn
your back
on them
they'll
descend
like a murder
of crows.

As soon as
you make
your presence
known, they'll
fan out in panic,
holding their
tongues,
pursued by
the greatest
of predators.

Awful Rumor,
mother of Shame,
was it Artemis
who made Ajax
attack the animals,
because of a victory
on the battlefield
or when he failed
to make sacrifices,
after slaying a deer,
stealing from her
the sacred honors
that she deserved?

Or did the war
gods plot against
him in the darkness,

contriving how
to stain his record?

Son of Telamon,
you must have
lost your mind
when you went
to war with cows!

Some god must
have infiltrated
your defenses,
infecting your head.

May Zeus and
Apollo silence
the rumor!

If Odysseus
and the generals,
who have smeared
many a reputation
in the past, are out
spreading lies
about you now,
I beg you, sir,
do not remain
in your tent
by the sea;
do not let them
say such things!

Make them look
you in the eye
and say it!

Rise up from the ground,
where you've remained
in silence for far too long,

allowing Rumor's fire
to consume your home,
while enemy whispers
whip up through the cracks
in the floorboards, fanning
the flames with their forked
tongues. Rise up now, sir,
or we're all going to burn!

TECMESSA *rushes out of the tent and*
falls to her knees before the CHORUS.

TECMESSA

Oh, you salt
of the earth,
you sailors
who serve
Ajax, those
of us who
care for
the house
of Telamon
will soon wail,
for our fierce
hero sits shell-
shocked in his
tent, glazed
over, gazing
into oblivion.

He has the thousand-yard stare.

CHORUS

What terrors
visited him
in the night

to reverse
his fortune
by morning?

Tell us, Tecmessa,
battle-won bride,
for no one is closer
to Ajax than you,
so you will speak
as one who knows.

TECMESSA

How can I say
something
that should never
be spoken?

You would
rather
die
than hear
what I'm
about to say.

A divine madness
poisoned his mind,
tainting his name
during the night.

Our home is
a slaughterhouse,
littered with cow
carcasses and
goats gushing
thick blood, throats
slit, horn to horn,
by his hand,

evil omens
of things to come.

CHORUS

Then it is true
what they say
about the hot-
headed man.

The great
story grows
louder and
louder with
each Greek
who tells it.

I'm afraid of what lies on the horizon.

He will die
when he looks
around and sees
what he has done,
for with his dark
sword and his mad
hand he has chopped
the herds and herds-
men into pieces.

TECMESSA *gestures toward the tent.*

TECMESSA

Over there,
over there,
that is where
he dragged
them, bound
with ropes.

He executed
some inside,
forcing them
to the ground;
the rest he tore
apart, savagely
scratching away
at their flanks
with his fingers.

With one quick
chop, he severed
the head of a white-
footed ram
and let it drop
to the floor,
then grabbing
another by the
throat, he tied
it down and
ripped out
its tongue,
then he lashed
it with his harsh
whip until there
was nothing
left to lash,
all the while
spewing vile
words that
must have
come from
a god.

The CHORUS *huddles together.*

CHORUS

> The time has come
> for us to hide
> our faces and run
> as far as we can,
> or board the ships
> and row wherever
> the ocean will allow;
> hounded by sharp
> words and hard
> stones hurled
> by the generals
> and their men,
> we must try to
> escape his fate!

TECMESSA *throws herself in front of the* CHORUS.

TECMESSA

> He has come back
> to his senses, and
> as a warm wind
> always follows
> the last lightning
> flash, his rage has
> been swept away
> only to reveal fresh
> wounds, for there
> is nothing more
> troubling for a man
> than to discover an
> evil crime of which
> he is the culprit.

CHORUS

> If the Fury
> has left him,
> then he will
> start to feel
> better soon,
> for the source
> of his suffering
> has vanished.

TECMESSA

> Tell me. Given
> the choice, which
> would you prefer:
> happiness while
> your friends are
> in pain or to share
> in their suffering?

CHORUS

> Twice the pain is twice as worse.

TECMESSA

> Then we'll get sick while he recovers.

CHORUS

> What do you mean?
> I do not follow the
> logic of your words.

TECMESSA

> In his madness
> he took pleasure

in the evil that
possessed him,
all the while
afflicting those
of us nearby,
but now that
the fever has
broken all of
his pleasure
has turned to
pain, and we
are still afflicted,
just as before.

Twice the pain is twice the sorrow.

CHORUS

I'm afraid that
some god struck
him down, for his
anguish grows as
his sanity returns.

TECMESSA

It is true, but still
hard to understand.

CHORUS

How did the madness
first take hold of him?
Tell us. We will stay
and share in the pain.

TECMESSA

Since your pain is now mine,
I will share this with you, too.

In the dead of night,
when the lamps no
longer burned, Ajax
found his sword and
moved for the door.

Naturally, I objected:
"Where are you going?
No messenger has come
calling for help. All of
the soldiers are asleep.
Please come back to bed."

He turned to me and
firmly said: "Woman,
silence becomes a
woman." I've heard
him say that before,
and I know what it
means, so I quit asking
questions, and he left
without saying a word.

Whatever happened
then I cannot say,
but soon he returned,
pulling bulls and sheep
tied up with ropes.

Dealing with some:
he lopped off their
heads, slit throats,
and snapped spines.

Others he tortured
as if they were men.

Finally, he dashed outside
and spoke to someone
in the shadows, cursing
the generals and Odysseus,
bragging and laughing
about sweet revenge.

He quickly returned
to the tent and slowly
returned to his senses.

When he finally saw
what he had done,
taking in the carnage,
he struck his head and
groaned like a bull,
diving onto the bodies,
rolling in their blood,
clawing at his face,
and tearing at his hair.
For a long time,
he sat in silence,
rocking on the floor,
but then wanted
to know what had
happened and
threatened to hurt
me if I didn't tell
him all that I knew.

I feared for my life
and quickly coughed
up the bitter story.

He started to make
these low sounds,
the kind I never
thought I'd hear
him make, for he
always told his men
that crying was for
women and cowards.

Tired from all the tears,
he now rests in his mess,
strangely silent, refusing
food or water, planning
to do some terrible thing.

I can hear it
in his voice.
That is why
I came to you!
Go inside
and see what
you can do!
Men will often
listen to friends!

CHORUS

Terrible are the evils
of which you spoke
that drove him mad.

> AJAX *groans, like a wounded animal,*
> *inside the tent.*

TECMESSA

I'm afraid things
will soon get worse!

Did you hear that low
groan rolling up
from Ajax's throat?

AJAX *groans louder.*

CHORUS

Either he must
be ill or is
made sick by
the thought
of his illness.

AJAX

My boy. Bring me my boy!

TECMESSA

Oh, god, no!
Where is he?
He wants to
see his boy,
Eurysaces.

AJAX

Teucer? Where is Teucer?
Always out raiding. I'm
in here dying! He's never
near when I need him most.

CHORUS

That is a sane
man's voice.
Open the door!
Perhaps he'll

snap out of it
with shame
when he sees
familiar faces.

TEMESSSA *opens the flaps of the tent to reveal* AJAX
sitting on a heap of animal corpses.

TECMESSA

There, they are open!

Now you can see him
as he is and look upon
the evil he has done.

AJAX *comes charging out of the tent.*

AJAX

You sailors! You
loyal friends, who
stood by me through
the worst of times,
do you see this wave
of destruction, full
of chum and guts,
crashing on all sides?

CHORUS (*to* TECMESSA)

Sadly, you were right.
He has come unhinged.

AJAX

You skilled sailors,
who joined me on
the open seas to row
against our enemies,

you are the only men
who can help me now.

Cut my throat right here,
right now, add me to this
pile. End my suffering!

CHORUS

Do not say these things.
We will not cure evil
with evil, for if we try,
the pain will only grow
worse than the illness
that brought it upon you.

AJAX

Do you see what
I have done? I was
the bravest in battle,
never lost my wits,
and now I've killed
these harmless barn-
yard animals with
my hands! What a joke
my life has become,
my reputation, my
sense of honor!

TECMESSA

Lord Ajax, I beg you
not to talk this way.

AJAX

Will you not leave me
alone, will you not go?
AAAAHHHHHHHH!

TECMESSA

> On my knees, please
> relent; use your head.

AJAX

> I was the one who let
> his enemies slip away
> and turned upon bulls
> and white goats to shed
> black blood in the night!

CHORUS

> What is done is done, sir.
> There's no changing the past.

AJAX

> You slick trickster,
> you cowardly fox,
> double-crossing
> arrogant Odysseus,
> I can hear your loud
> laughter rattling in
> my skull, mocking
> me for this mistake.

CHORUS

> The gods say when
> men laugh and cry.

AJAX

> If I could only look
> him in the eye, even
> though I am destroyed.

CHORUS

Swallow your proud
words, sir! Don't you
see the quicksand
in which we now stand?

AJAX

Zeus. Father of my
forefathers, let me
kill that man of many
turns, the one I hate,
along with the brother-
kings, then let me die.

TECMESSA

Pray for my death,
too. I will not live
when you are dead!

AJAX

Darkness,
my light,
black abyss,
take me
down to
live in
oblivion,
for I am
no longer
worthy to
live among
gods or men.

Athena,
gray-eyed

goddess,
daughter
of Zeus,
will torture
me until
I'm dead.

Nowhere
to run,
no escape.

My greatness
dies on this
heap of beasts.

I defeated
myself with
delusions.

TECMESSA (*through her teeth*)

It's hard to hear a strong
man say such weak words!

AJAX

You surging straits,
roaring with waves,
you caves, you groves
along the coast, you
have held me at Troy
for many long years,
no longer, no longer,
when I have ceased to
fill my lungs with air.

AJAX *briefly turns to* TECMESSA,
her words still stinging . . .

I speak to those who understand!

You river streams
of Scamander,
killer of Greeks,
you shall never
see my face again
in your waters.
I will say it plainly:
the face of the best
warrior ever to be
seen in Troy, who
came from Greece
and now lies here,
wallowing in filth,
stripped of all honor.

CHORUS (*to* TECMESSA)

It's not for me
to say if you
should hold
back or go
on this way,
having seen
the evil things
you've seen.

AJAX (*moaning his own name*)

Ajax!
Ajax!

My name is a sad song.

Who would
have thought

it would some-
day become
the sound a man
makes in despair?

Ajax!

After sacking Troy,
my father, Telamon,
rode home in
a victory parade.

He made quite a name
for himself here in this
country, receiving full
honors from the army.

But now I, the son,
stand in the place
where my father
once stood, with
no less troops and
no fewer triumphs,
but my body will rot
on strange soil, dis-
honored in front
of fellow soldiers.

This much I know:
if Achilles still lived
and decided to hold
a contest for his arms,
awarding them to
the greatest warrior,
at the end of the day
they would be mine,
but the generals gave
the arms to a man with-

out morals, ignoring all
the times I risked my
life to defend them
against our enemies,
and if my eyes and mind
had not been twisted by
a sickness, taking me off
target, the generals and
Odysseus would not have
lived to cast their votes,
let alone see the morning,
but the relentless, dark-
eyed daughter of Zeus
ravaged me with madness
as I stood beside their beds,
and I stained my hands
with the blood of cows.

The men I hunted
down narrowly escaped.

Through no fault
of mine, they laugh
at me, for with a god's
help, the weak
evaded the strong.

What should I do now?

The gods hate me,
the Greeks loathe me,
the Trojans despise me.

Perhaps I should set
sail for home, across
the open sea, leaving
behind ships and men,

and the sons of Atreus?
But what will I say
to my father, Telamon,
when he sees my face?

How will he even bear
to look at me when I
explain how I disgraced
our family name for
which he fought so hard?

His heart will break
right then and there.

Should I scale the walls
of Troy and face the army
by myself, show them what
I'm made of, and then die?

No, that would only
please the generals.

I must do something
bold to erase all doubt
in my father's mind
that his son was any-
thing but a coward.

When a man suffers
without end in sight
and takes no pleasure
in living his life, day
by day wishing for
death, he should not
live out all his years.

It is pitiful when men
hold on to false hopes.
A great man must

live in honor or die
an honorable death.

That is all I have to say.

CHORUS

No one will ever say
that what you just said
was spoken by anyone
other than you, Ajax.
Your words were true
to your heart and spirit.
But, just for a moment,
release your thoughts
and listen to what those
who love you have to say.

TECMESSA *approaches* AJAX,
her head bowed.

TECMESSA

Lord Ajax, there is nothing
worse in this world for men
than the necessity of Fate.

I came from a wealthy family.
My father was the richest man
in Phrygia; now I am a slave.

The gods willed
that you would
win me with your
strength, and I have
accepted my destiny
of sharing your bed
and have come
with time to love
you very much,

and so I beg you,
by our home and
by the bed we share,
do not let me suffer
at the hands of your
enemies, do not turn
me over to the men
whom you hate, for
on the day you die,
moments after your
death, your son and I
will be snatched up
by the Greeks and
treated like slaves.

One of my new masters
will sneer at me and say:
"Look. There is that
woman, the mistress
of Ajax, the strongest
warrior in the entire
army. Can you actually
believe that people
used to envy her?
She is nothing now
but a common slave."

That's what he'll say,
and worse. And the pain
of it will be my fate,
and the shame of it
will stain your family.

Think about your father,
whom you will be
abandoning in the throes
of old age, and your poor

old mother, who spends
all of her days praying
that you will some day
return home alive.

And what about your son?

Can you imagine how hard
your death will be on him,
growing up fatherless and
without food on the table,
living with men who hate
him for being your son?

I have nowhere else to go,
no one to whom I can turn.

My parents are dead.
You destroyed my
homeland. You now
are my homeland,
my safety, my life.

Nothing else matters but you!

I ask you to remember
all the good times
we had and to treat
me kindly, for a noble
man always remembers
those who gave him
pleasure and protects
them from danger.

CHORUS

I hope you will
pity this woman,
and welcome her
words, as we do.

AJAX

> I will welcome her
> when she has done
> as she's been told.

TECMESSA

> My dear Ajax,
> I shall always
> do as you say.

AJAX

> Then bring me my
> boy, so I can see him!

TECMESSA

> Forgive me, sir,
> I hid him in fear.

AJAX

> Were you afraid he
> would see his father
> covered in blood?

TECMESSA (*not backing down*)

> I was afraid
> he would lose
> his life if you
> laid eyes on him!

AJAX

> I suppose that was right,
> given the state I was in.

TECMESSA

> I tried my best to keep
> him out of harm's way.

AJAX

> I approve of your actions.
> You showed great foresight.

TECMESSA

> Oh, my sweet Ajax,
> what can I do to make
> things better between us?

AJAX

> Let me see my boy.
>
> Let me speak with
> him, man-to-man.

TECMESSA

> He is guarded nearby.

AJAX (*softly*)

> Why am I made
> to wait for him?

TECMESSA

> Eurysaces, your father
> calls you. It's all right,
> there's nothing to fear.

> > EURYSACES *runs to* TECMESSA *and*
> > *hides in her arms.*

AJAX

> Lift him up to me,
> that's right, lift him
> up right here, he
> won't be afraid
> of freshly spilled
> blood, not my boy.

> > TECMESSA *passes* EURYSACES *to* AJAX.

> A father must expose
> his son to things like
> this, toughen him
> up, mold his nature.

> My dear boy, may
> you have better luck
> than your father, but
> come to resemble
> him in all other ways,
> especially bravery.

> I envy you, son,
> for you are
> far too young
> to apprehend
> the evil that
> surrounds us.

> Ignorance is bliss,
> before you know
> pleasure and pain.

> But when you grow
> up, your enemies
> will see your father
> in your actions.

> Until then, I want you
> to enjoy being a boy,

play in the warm breeze,
make your mother smile.

None of the Greeks
will insult you or mis-
treat you, though you
will be fatherless. I will
leave you to the care of
my half brother, Teucer,
to raise you to be a man.
He isn't afraid to hunt
his enemies, even if he's
never around when
I need him the most.

AJAX *addresses the* CHORUS.

You loyal sailors,
who fought along-
side me with your
thick shields to hold
back our enemies
on the battle lines,
you will now report
to Teucer. Stand by
him as he brings my
boy to see my father,
Telamon, and my
mother, Eriboea, so
he may look after them
as they slowly decline
into the darkness below.

And hear this clearly!

No man shall
ever touch
my arms,

or win them
in a contest
after I am gone!

They will not
be taken by
the Greeks, or
by the thief who
stole my honor!

They now belong to my boy,
after which he was named.

That's right, son. Eurysaces
means "strong shield." That's
what you are destined to be.

So take what is rightfully
yours and carry it with you
always. It is your namesake,
my unbreakable shield, sewn
from the hides of seven bulls.

The rest of the arms will
be buried with my body!

Take him away from me
and lock the doors. Now!
And hold back your tears.
This is no time for crying.
Go inside, shut the gates,
before I lose my nerve!

CHORUS

It scares me to hear
you speak with such
an edge in your voice.

TECMESSA

> I know that tone,
> Ajax. What evil
> thing are you
> planning to do?

AJAX

> No more questions.
> Silence is best.
> Show some restraint.

TECMESSA

> By our son and by
> the gods, I now
> grovel at your feet:
> please, please,
> do not abandon us.

AJAX

> Do not talk about the gods.
> I owe them nothing now.

TECMESSA

> Do not curse yourself.

AJAX

> Save it for those
> who will listen.

TECMESSA

> Will you not listen?

AJAX

> You have already said too much.

TECMESSA

Out of fear, my lord.

AJAX

Shut the gates, woman!

TECMESSA

For gods' sake, back down!

AJAX

It's far
too late
to shape
my nature.
Don't be stupid.
Leave me alone!

> TECMESSA *grabs* EURYSACES *and*
> *carries him into the tent.*
> AJAX *follows them inside and closes the flaps.*
> *Finally alone, the* CHORUS *debates what to do.*

CHORUS

Salamis, our famous
wave-beaten home,
shelter from storms,
bright white beacon
over the ocean, surely
you are still out there,
the same as when
we left for this god-
forsaken place.

I've grown so home-
sick over these months
encamped on the out-

skirts of Troy, worn
down by the tortures
of time, waiting here
to die and someday
set foot on the black
dust of Hades' shores.

And now I must care
for incurable Ajax,
his mind infected
by divine madness.

He was the one you
sent overseas to win
the war with over-
whelming force.

Now he is alone.

Caught up
in thoughts,
he unnerves
his friends,
as we watch
his greatest
acts of bravery
slip through his
fingers, only
to be forgotten,
erased from history
by the generals.

When his poor mother,
weathered with age,
whitened by time,
hears how her son
was addled
by a madness

which ravaged his
mind, there will be
no shortage of high-
pitched cries piercing
our eardrums as she
shrieks his funeral song,
pounding her breasts
with her fists and
tearing out clumps
of long white hair.

The suffering patient
who lives on with end-
less affliction is better
when he rests in Hades.

He who was born
to become one of
the greatest Greek
warriors now turns
on himself in anger.

His brokenhearted
father will soon
struggle under
the weight of what
remains of his son,
who was singled out
for self-annihilation.

                   AJAX *appears, carrying a sword,*
                              followed by TECMESSA.

AJAX

    Great mysterious
    Time reveals and

conceals all things:
darkness into light,
light into darkness.

Nothing is beyond its reach.

Curses sworn
in wild rage
are reversed;
iron wills bend.

Even I, who
just moments
ago, stood un-
movable am
now moved
by the words
of this woman.

I do not wish
to leave her
a widow, or
abandon my
boy at the feet
of enemies.

I shall scrub
off this grime
in the salt
marshes
by the sea,
cleanse
away
the goddess'
rage.

Then, I will find
virgin earth in which
to bury this sword,

worst of all weapons,
where no one will
look upon it again,
engulfed in shadows,
protected in Hades.

It was a gift from
my deadliest enemy.

Hector.

The saying is true:
the gifts of enemies
are never gifts.

In time, I will yield
to the gods and learn
to obey the generals.

They are my superiors,
and, as a soldier, I must
follow their orders.

Even the most powerful
forces in nature submit
themselves to authority.

Winter blizzards melt
away in summer heat.

The swirling vortex
of Night makes
way for the stark
white chariot of Day.

A howling gale quiets
the giant ocean waves.

All-subsuming Sleep
holds men in its spell,
only to release them
in the morning.

I must learn balance,
for I now know that
the enemies we hate
may one day become
our closest of friends.

And from now on
I shall help friends
without forgetting
that in this world
men rarely remain
friends and often
become enemies.

Friendship
is a dangerous
harbor for
most men.

These things will
all work out for
the best in the end.

Go inside,
woman, pray
to the gods
that I will
achieve what
I have in my
heart to do.

TECMESSA *hesitates, then goes inside the tent.*

Pray with her,
friends, and
when Teucer
comes, relay
these orders:
look after me

and be loyal
to you in all
ways. I will
now go where
I must go. Do
as I've asked
and you will
see that as un-
lucky as I have
been today, I
am now saved.

AJAX *walks down the road,*
carrying the sword of Hector.

CHORUS

I am intoxicated
by sweet desire.

Floating.

My feet may
never touch the
ground again.

Pan, Pan,
stretch out
over the wide
ocean from
the white-
capped peaks
of Cyllene.

Pan, Pan, god
who leads the
dancing of
the gods, fill us
up with ecstasy,

whirl within us,
dance the sacred
steps you taught
yourself so long
ago in Mysia
and Knossos.

I want to dance
until Apollo, lord
of Delos, crosses
the Icarian Sea
in all his glory, to
dance inside of me.

The war god
has wiped
the terror
from my eyes.

Zeus, Zeus,
the bright white
light of Day
now shines upon
our swift ships,
as Ajax puts
aside his pain
and travels
to the shore,
in reverence
for the gods,
to make
sacrifices.

Great Time
encompasses
all things.

Nothing is
impossible
if Ajax can
extinguish
his slow-
burning
hatred
for the sons
of Atreus.

> The MESSENGER *abruptly appears.*

MESSENGER

I have news, friends!

Teucer is back
from the Mysian
hills, but when
he descended
to the base camp
the men began
to swarm around
him, cursing his
name, spitting at
his feet. They took
turns abusing him:
saying he was the
half brother of a
madman, a traitor
who tried to take
down the army;
the soldiers would
not be satisfied until
they saw his body
riddled with wounds,

rotting above earth,
exposed to the sun's
slow-roasting heat.

Swords were drawn.

It would have ended
badly had the officers
not put it to rest.
But where is Ajax?

I have news for him.

A man must report
all that he knows
to those in command.

CHORUS

He was just here,
but now he is gone,
a new man with
fresh intentions.

MESSENGER

Then I am either
too late or too
slow. Either way,
I have failed.

CHORUS

Too late for what?

MESSENGER

Teucer said
that Ajax
must stay
inside until
he arrives.

CHORUS

> Do not worry.
> He has gone
> to make
> peace with
> the gods
> who stoked
> his rage.

MESSENGER

> Your words
> are worthless
> if Calchas
> truly sees.

CHORUS

> What do you know?
> And what have you
> come here to say?

MESSENGER

> This is what I know.
>
> Calchas
> moved away
> from the men
> who flanked
> the generals
> and motioned,
> with one hand,
> for Teucer
> to join him.
>
> If he ever wished to see
> his brother again, said
> Calchas, he would stop

at nothing to keep Ajax
from leaving his tent
today, for the savage
Fury of goddess Athena
will hound him for only
one day, and no more.

Then he spoke
the following
words, making
sure each word
was understood:

"The gods destroy
men whose bodies
blur the distinction
between gods and men,
or who think they can
outthink the gods."

His father warned
him, as he rushed
off to war, not to be
careless or stupid:

"My son, always
hope to win, but
only with help
from the gods."

But Ajax turned
back and boasted:

"Father, no man
wins when gods
are involved. No
doubt, I can win
without them."

That is what he said.

And then when
Athena ordered
him to slaughter
the Trojans in
battle, he turned
to her and said:

"Lady, step aside.
Stand over there
with the rest of
the Greeks. This
battle line will not
break while I am
holding it down."

With these words
he won the hatred
of the goddess.

But if he some-
how makes it
through this day,
we may be able
to save him
from himself.

So spoke Calchas.

I was sent here by Teucer.

These were my orders.

If we are too late,
then Ajax is dead.

CHORUS (*shouts into the tent*)

> Tecmessa!
>
> You who were
> born for nothing
> but pain, come
> out of the tent,
> hear this man's
> story; his words
> cut too close
> and too deep
> to be ignored.

> TECMESSA *rushes out of the tent,*
> *carrying* EURYSACES.

TECMESSA

> Have I not suffered
> enough today?
>
> Why have you called
> me out of the tent?
>
> I was finally going
> to rest my weary eyes
> when I heard your
> loud shouting.

CHORUS

> Listen to this man's
> news about Ajax and
> you will understand why
> I cried your name.

TECMESSA

> What are you going to say?
> Is it over? Are we lost?

MESSENGER

> That is not for me
> to say, but I can tell
> you this: Ajax must
> not leave his tent today.

TECMESSA

> He is outside.
>
> Why do I fear
> your words?

MESSENGER

> Teucer sent me
> with strict orders:
>
> "Keep him inside
> the tent and do
> not allow him
> to go out alone."

TECMESSA

> Where is Teucer?
> Why did he say this?

MESSENGER

> He just returned
> and has reason
> to believe that
> if Ajax steps out-
> side his tent, his
> life will be over.

TECMESSA

> And from whom
> did he learn this?

MESSENGER

> From Calchas,
> the seer, who says
> this day brings life
> or death for Ajax.

TECMESSA

> Is this the necessity of Fate?
>
> Men, please protect us.
> You: go find Teucer. Now!
>
> The rest
> of you,
> split up—
> go east
> and west,
> search the
> shoreline,
> find out
> where
> his evil
> intentions
> have taken
> him.

> *The* CHORUS *splits into small units that
> sprint for the dunes in search of* AJAX.

> I now see.
>
> He had me
> fooled, but
> now I see.
>
> I have been
> cast aside,
> discarded

from his
grieving
heart
forever.

Son, what should I do?
I can't just wait
here, helplessly.

I must run, as
far as my legs
will carry me.

> TECMESSA *leads* EURYSACES *inside and*
> *runs after the* CHORUS.

There's no time to waste
when a man wants to die!

> AJAX *steps into a small pool of light.*
> *He is alone on a dune, no one for miles.*
> *He takes the sword of Hector and buries it,*
> *blade up, in the sand.*

AJAX

The killer now
stands where it
will cut the best,
in enemy soil,
a gift from Hector,
my mortal enemy,
recently sharpened
on an iron-grinding
stone, now packed
firmly in the earth,
so it will deliver a
quick and easy death.

All set.

I call upon Zeus,
father of my forefathers,
only to ask one thing:
that the news of my
death is delivered to
Teucer, so he may
be the first to see me
covered in blood,
having fallen upon
this sharp sword,
and so that I may
not be discovered
by enemies, who
will feed my body
to vultures and dogs.

This is all I ask.

I call out to Hermes,
escort of the dead,
who delivers men
to the underworld,
to guide this sword
as it pierces my rib
cage so it skewers
my heart and ends
my life instantly,
sparing me pain
after the plunge.

I call upon the Furies,
those long-striding
dread maidens who
avenge humans and
see to their endless
suffering: witness

how the generals
have destroyed me!

Train your eyes on
those evil men,
snatch them with
your talons and,
just as I die at
my own hands,
may they also be
murdered by their
own flesh and blood.

It's feeding time!

Gorge yourselves
on the generals
and their men;
fiercely descend
upon the army;
devour it whole;
spare no soldier!

I call out to you, Helios,
as your burning chariot
streaks across the sky,
when you come to my
home, pull back your
blazing reins and pause
to announce my death
to my poor old father
and to the pitiful woman
who nursed me as a child.

No doubt, when she hears
the news, her wailing will
be heard through the hills.

No more talk of tears.
It's time.

Death, oh, Death,
come now and
visit me . . .

But I shall miss
the light of day
and the sacred
fields of Salamis,
where I played as
a boy, and great
Athens, and all
my friends.

I call out to you,
springs and rivers
fields and plains,
who nourished me
during these long
years at Troy.

These are the last
words you will
hear Ajax speak . . .

AJAX *impales himself on the sword and gasps for air.*

The rest I shall say
to those who listen
in the world below.

AJAX *dies.*
The CHORUS *searches frantically for* AJAX.

CHORUS 1

We've been
searching
and searching,

up and down
the shoreline,
but he is
nowhere,
nowhere,
nowhere,
to be found.

Listen, listen.
I hear a noise.

CHORUS 2

It's only us.

CHORUS 1

What's the status?

CHORUS 2

We swept the area
west of the ships.

CHORUS 1

Any sign?

CHORUS 2

None.

CHORUS 1

We scoured
the eastern
zone, but
saw nothing.

CHORUS 2

If only a hard-
working fisherman,

wide-eyed
and awake,
or an Olympian
nymph, or one
of the quick-
flowing rivers
of the Bosporus,
could tell us
where to find
him, as he
wanders
these beaches,
sullen and alone.

I'm tired
of running
in circles
after this
afflicted man.

TECMESSA *discovers* AJAX's *body and howls in*
anguish, an inhuman cry.

CHORUS

What was that sound
coming from the trees?

TECMESSA

Wretched!
I am wretched!

The CHORUS *spots* TECMESSA *and runs to her side.*

CHORUS

I see the battle-
won bride over-
come with grief.

TECMESSA

> It's over, friends.
> Everything is lost.

CHORUS

> What is it?

TECMESSA

> Ajax, freshly
> dead, impaled
> on his sword.

CHORUS

> There will be
> no more hope
> of homecoming.

> He has killed us
> with his death.

> We'll be dead
> upon arrival,
> coming back
> in body bags.

> Poor woman.

TECMESSA

> He has died and
> we must weep.

CHORUS

> By whose hand
> did he go down?

TECMESSA

> By his own.
> Look at how
> the sword juts
> out of the earth.

CHORUS

> How could
> I have been
> so blind, so deaf
> to your cries,
> while the red
> blood gushed
> from a hole
> in your chest?
>
> Where is he?
> Where is un-
> bending Ajax,
> whose name is now
> a sad, sad song?

TECMESSA

> He is not to be seen!
> I will cover his body
> with this white cloth.
> for no one who loved
> him could bear to see
> the black blood drip
> from his nostrils and
> the deep, self-inflicted
> wound, a gaping hole
> at the center of his chest.

TECMESSA *covers* AJAX *with a cloth.*

What am I to do now?
Which of you will lift
him? Where is Teucer?
He should be here now
to help prepare the body
for a proper burial. We
don't have much time.
Oh, Ajax, this was no
way to die, not for you.
Even your enemies will
weep when they see you.

CHORUS

It was just a matter
of time before you
ended your pain by
taking your own life.

Horrible thoughts
coursed through your
head while bitter
words spewed
from your mouth,
fueled by ever-
lasting hatred for
the sons of Atreus.

TECMESSA (*sobbing*)

Why me?

CHORUS

Her grief
pierces

deeper
than I ever
imagined.

TECMESSA (*sobbing*)

Why me?
Why me?

CHORUS

It's hard to hear
you crying, but
understandable
after such a loss.

TECMESSA

You can try
to imagine
how I must
feel, but I am
the one who
must feel it.

CHORUS

We know.

TECMESSA

My son, we will
soon be slaves
to cruel masters.

CHORUS

No!

Please do not
think such
evil thoughts.

The sons
of Atreus
will not add
to your misery.

A god will intervene.

TECMESSA

Is this not the work of a god?

CHORUS

Yes, and the weight
of it is hard to bear.

TECMESSA

Awful Athena,
daughter of Zeus,
makes us suffer
to please her
dear Odysseus.

CHORUS

The man of many
turns now mocks
our suffering; he's
laughing at us, along
with the generals.

TECMESSA

Let him laugh.
Let them all laugh.

They won't laugh
for long, when
they lack his
shield in combat.

Evil men only
appreciate good
men, like Ajax,
after they're gone.

His death is as bitter
to me as it is sweet
to them and blissful
for him, for he died
according to his wishes.

They have no reason
to claim victory over
him. It was a god who
took his life, not them!

Let Odysseus curse
his name and hurl
hard words. Ajax
won't hear them.

He is gone, far away
from here. He knows
neither their laughter
nor my loud moans.

TEUCER *suddenly appears on the edge
of the crowd and, overcome with grief,
lets out a low, ominous moan.*

CHORUS

Silence.

I hear
the voice
of Teucer.

His cry cuts
straight
to the heart
of our pain.

TEUCER

Dearest Ajax,
whose blood
courses through
my veins, what
have you done?

Tell me
the rumor
isn't true.

CHORUS

Know this, Teucer:
the man is dead.

TEUCER

So this is my fate.

CHORUS

This is our fate.

TEUCER

I'm wretched. Wretched.

CHORUS

> We groan with you.

TEUCER

> My heart is broken.

CHORUS

> Our hearts are broken, too.

TEUCER

> But what about his boy,
> his son, where is he now?

CHORUS

> Alone by the camp.

TEUCER

> Get him, right now,
> bring him here or an
> enemy will snatch
> him up like a lion
> cub ripped from its
> mother's den. Go!
> Don't delay another
> second. Evil men
> love to kick corpses.

> TECMESSA *rushes back to the camp.*

CHORUS

> Well done,
> Teucer. His
> final orders
> were for you

to look after
his family.

TEUCER

Of all the things
my eyes have
ever seen, this
burns the worst.

No other road
has wounded
me as deeply
as this one.

What began
as a search-
and-rescue
mission has
now ended
in a funeral
procession.

The story
of your
death shot
quickly
through
the camps,
reaching
my ears
before I
reached
your body.

When I heard
the news,

I doubled over,
sick to my
stomach,
holding in
the black bile
welling with-
in me, but now
that I see what
you have done,
I can't hold it
in any longer.

Uncover him!
Let me see it all!

The CHORUS *uncovers* AJAX.

Look at that
face, his face
says everything:
the suffering,
the bitterness,
the courage,
the misery.

What terrors
await me now
that you're dead?

Where can I show
my face, among
what men—when
I was not where
I should have been
when you needed
me the most?

(*with bitter sarcasm*)

Our father,
Telamon,
will no doubt
greet me with
open arms
when I return
home with-
out you.

Of course,
the man
never let
on when
he was
pleased,
even when
luck fell in
his favor.

Far be it from
him to show
his emotions.

But in the silence
of your absence
when it finally
all sinks in, what
vile words will
not cross his lips
as he slings them
in my direction?

He will call
me a bastard
son of a battle-
won bride, a
weak, worth-

less good-for-
nothing traitor,
the one who
let you down,
dear Ajax, and
left you for dead,
deceitfully, so
I could one day
command your
men and rule
over your home.

Our bitter old
father will say
these hateful
things, for he
is hotheaded,
quick-fisted,
and fast to
pick a fight
with anyone,
over nothing,
in his old age.

In the end,
he'll throw
me out of
the house,
disowning
me as his
son, calling
me a slave.

That's what
I have to look
forward to at
home, but here

at Troy, I am
surrounded by
enemies with
no hope of
anyone's help.

All my defenses
died with you.

And so, what
should I do?

How am I
supposed
to pull this
weapon from
your chest,
the one
that ended
your breath?

I wonder
if you fore-
saw how
Hector
would slay
you from
the grave?

CHORUS

No more words.
It's time to bury
this man before
time runs out.

I see an enemy
fast approaching,

a small-minded
man who laughs
at our suffering.

> *The* CHORUS *crowds around* AJAX *and*
> *hoists his body in the air.*

TEUCER

Which officer
do you see?

CHORUS

Menelaus,
for whom
the war
was fought.

TEUCER

I see him, too.

He's hard
to miss
from only
a few
feet away.

> MENELAUS *appears, rushing toward* TEUCER
> *and the* CHORUS.

MENELAUS

Put that body down.
That's a direct order.

TEUCER

Those are big
words from
a small man.

MENELAUS

My orders are
nonnegotiable.

They come from
a superior officer,
the commander
of the army.

TEUCER

On what grounds?

MENELAUS

We were under
the mistaken
impression that
he was our friend
when we brought
him to Troy.

Now we have found
him to be worse than
our enemies, a cold-
blooded killer who
crept upon our beds
at night with hunger
for blood. And had
a goddess not held
back his hand, we'd
be cold corpses
splayed out on
the floor, and he'd
be the last man
standing, laughing
at us. But as Fate
would have it, a

goddess deflected
his attack and sent
him off to slaughter
barnyard animals.

There is no man
in the world who
is strong enough
to bury this body.

He was an outcast
and therefore we
shall cast out his
carcass on
the yellow sands
of foreign shores as
food for scavenging
birds and dogs.

Do not think
of defying us.

Though he never
obeyed orders
or listened to
a word I said
when he was
still living, we
shall bend him
to our will, now
that he is dead.

Insubordination
is the sign of
a weak mind.

There is no law
in a city where

there is no
fear of the law.

The army dis-
integrates when
men no longer
fear or respect
their superiors.

A giant can
always slip on
a small stone.

A soldier who
feels fear and
shame is often
safe from harm.

But a soldier
who breaks
rules and rank
punctures the hull
of a smooth-
sailing ship and
scuttles it along
the ocean floor.

Terror has a rightful
place in our society.

We should not
act according to
our pleasure and
not expect pain
in equal measure.

They are two sides
of the same coin.

A few hours ago,
this man was swollen
with self-regard.

It is my turn now.

You will not bury
this body, unless
you wish to dig
your own grave.

CHORUS

Menelaus, you have said
many wise things about
temperance and pride.

Practice what you preach.
Do not disgrace the dead.

TEUCER

There is something
wrong when a man
who comes from
nothing is slandered
by a man who comes
from supposedly
noble parents.

For the record, you
say you personally
brought him here as
an ally of the army?

But didn't he sail
on his own accord?

At what point did
you become his
superior, ruling

over the sailors
he brought here
from his home?

You may be the king
of Sparta, but that
means nothing to us.

You had no right
to order him around,
no more than he had
to tell you what to do.

You sailed here as
a subordinate. What
makes you think
you outrank Ajax?

Go bark orders
at your soldiers,
lash them with
your harsh tongue.

But know this:
your words do
not frighten me.

I'm going to bury
my commander.

It is only right,
for he did not
risk his life for
the sake of your
wife, but came
here on account
of oaths he had
sworn to uphold,
not to you, since

it is impossible
to swear an oath
to a man who
has no values.

Go ahead, call
your commander,
if you like, I'll
never back down,
especially when
threatened by
a man like you.

CHORUS

Times are hard
enough without
bitter words
between allies.

Even if they are justified,
they cut close to the bone.

MENELAUS

Look. The archer
is proud of himself.

TEUCER

I'm not embarrassed of my bow.

MENELAUS

Your bragging would grow
louder, if you still had a shield.

TEUCER

I could take you down
without a shield, even if
you were fully armed.

MENELAUS

> Your heart
> is feeding
> arrogant
> words to
> your tongue.

TEUCER

> I speak proud words,
> but they are also just.

MENELAUS

> Is it just to defend
> a cold-blooded killer?

TEUCER

> Whom did he kill,
> other than himself?

MENELAUS

> He tried to kill me,
> but a god intervened.

TEUCER

> You dishonor the gods
> with your unjust actions.

MENELAUS

> And what divine
> law have I broken?

TEUCER

> Exposing a dead
> man's body to

the elements,
denying it a
proper burial.

MENELAUS

The body of an enemy
never deserves burial.

TEUCER

When did Ajax
fight you in battle?

MENELAUS

We despised
each other,
as you know.

TEUCER

You provoked
him when you
fixed the vote.

MENELAUS

The judges voted.
He lost the count.

TEUCER

Spoken like a
true politician.

MENELAUS

Your words sting,
but they will soon
bring you pain.

TEUCER

> No more for me
> than for you.

MENELAUS

> I will only say it
> one more time:
> this man is not
> to be buried.

TEUCER

> And you will only hear
> me say it once again:
> this man will be buried.

MENELAUS

> I once heard about
> a captain who spoke
> loud, forceful words
> to spur his men to sail
> into a storm, but when
> the ship was being ripped
> apart by waves and wind,
> the captain quietly took
> cover under a tarp and
> was trampled by his men.
>
> Be careful. A powerful
> storm may just descend
> from a small cloud and
> silence your shouting.

TEUCER

> And I once saw
> a churlish man

pick a fight at
a funeral, and some-
one like me took
him aside and said:
"Do not desecrate
the dead, sir, for if
you do, you will
suffer greatly for it."

MENELAUS

That's it. It's shameful
to trade insults with an
inferior man. Why use
words? I can use force.

TEUCER

Go then!
It's shameful
to listen to your
meaningless
speeches.

MENELAUS *sprints off to find his brother.*

CHORUS

Dark clouds
are brewing on
the horizon, fed
by this fighting.

Teucer, you must
dig a quick trench
and bury this man
in the hollow earth,
where his body may

Ajax · 103

rest and his myth may
always be remembered.

TECMESSA *returns with* EURYSACES.

TEUCER

Look. His beloved
son and wife are here
just in time to chant
the sacred funeral
songs and dispose
of what remains.

Son, stand right here
and hold on to your father.
And here, hold these three
locks of hair—mine, yours,
and your mother's, for this
is what a suppliant must do.

And if any soldier attempts
to pull you away from this
corpse, may that man die,
abandoned by his friends,
and then rot above the earth!

I say this as I cut my hair.

Hold on, son. Stand guard.
And no matter what happens,
do not allow him to be moved.

TEUCER *addresses the* CHORUS.

Men, remember your orders!
Do not act like girls. Defend
this corpse with your lives
until I return. I will go dig

a hole in the ground, even
if they call me a criminal.

TEUCER *sprints away to find a place*
to bury his brother.

CHORUS

How many years
will it take for my
wandering to end,
and when will this
relentless battle
on the outskirts
of Troy with its
countless terrors
and unending
violence finally
come to an end,
even if it means
the Greeks will
be defeated?

I wish the Man
behind it all,
the Architect
of War, had
vanished or
perished before
he gave us
the tools to kill
and taught us
how to use them.

He has robbed
me of flowers

and large bowls
of wine, and
the sound of
sweet music.

He has destroyed
my friendships,
taken away my
ability to sleep,
and cut off my
heart from all
feeling, numbing
me to love or
being loved.
He has left me
out in the cold
waiting to die,
lost and shivering
on distant shores.

I used to feel safe
from covert attacks
and night terrors,
when Ajax still
lived and served
as my shield.

But now that he lies
here dead on the ground,
what happiness is left
for me in this world?

I wish I were standing
on the thick-wooded
cliff of Cape Sounion,
which overlooks the sea,

so could I shout hello
to sacred Athens.

TEUCER *suddenly returns.*

TEUCER

I decided to double back
when I saw Agamemnon
across the dunes, moving
in this direction, ready
to assault us with harsh
words upon his arrival.

AGAMEMNON *appears.*

AGAMEMNON

You there!
Is it true what I hear?

That you openly
disrespected your
commanders with
belligerent words
that so far have
gone unpunished?

Was it really you,
the son of a slave,
who said these
arrogant things?

Had you been born
of a noble family,
who knows, you
might have even
looked down at us,

as you walked on
the tips of your toes.

So what does all of this
empty talk accomplish,
a man who came from
nothing, defending a man
who amounted to nothing?

You have publicly
proclaimed that we
are not your superior
officers, nor captains
of the fleet, with power
to command the Greeks
or give orders to your men.

You say that Ajax sailed
as his own commander.

This is the kind
of outrageous
remark we often
hear from slaves.

Who was this man
whom you defend
with proud words?

What was he made of?

Where did he stand
in battle where I did
not stand beside him?

Was he the only
warrior in the army?

Oh, it was a dark day
when we announced

the competition for
Achilles' armor, for
it was the day when
Teucer decided—
once and for all—
that we were evil,
corrupt to the core,
and that he would
never accept our
judges' decisions
or concede his
brother's defeat.

Instead, you sneak up
from behind the lines
to pelt us with insults
and stab us in the back.

The rule of law will
fall apart if we subvert
our judges' decisions,
making winners losers
and losers winners,
to appease the bitter
anger of those who lost.

No. This must be stopped.

In the end, a quick mind
always trumps a broad chest.

A large ox cuts an even
line along the road when
driven by a small whip.

And since we're on the
subject of whipping . . .

I think you know where
I'm headed, if you don't

come to your senses
and cease howling
about a man who isn't
here, a shadow, a ghost.

Show some intelligence,
Teucer, know your place,
and next time, be sure to
bring along an interpreter,
as I can barely make out
your primitive language.

CHORUS

I wish you both would be reasonable.
I have nothing more to say than this.

TEUCER

Oh, how quickly
we forget. Right
after a man dies,
gratitude instantly
evaporates into a
cloud of betrayal.

How many times
did he put his life
on the line for you,
shielding you from
enemy attacks?

All gone.

No more memory
of Ajax, cast out
with his corpse.

Do you actually
not recall when

you were pinned
against a wall by
enemy fire, your
forces reduced
to nearly nothing?

As the flames
spread from ship
to ship, mighty
Hector leaped over
the hulls and on
to your deck with
every intention of
taking you down.

Tell me!
Who saved you that day?
Was it some base criminal?

And who faced
Hector head-on
and hand-to-hand,
of his own free will,
after drawing lots?

Clearly you don't
remember how he
cast the heaviest
coin into the pot
so as to ensure
that he would be
the one to fight.

That's just the kind of man he was.

It was he who did this!
I was there by his side,
the so-called slave,
the son of a foreigner!

How dare you speak
to me this way, when
everyone knows that
your father's father,
Pelops, was Phrygian?

And what about Atreus,
the man who gave you life,
who murdered his brother's
children and then served him
their flesh, nicely carved
on a platter, an unholy feast?

Your mother was a Cretan,
who was caught making
love with a stranger and
then thrown by your father
to the sharks in the ocean.

You actually insult me,
the son of Telamon,
who as a soldier won
my mother, the princess
daughter of Laomedon,
as a prize for his valor,
bestowed by Heracles.

I am the noble son of noble parents!

How could I allow
a man who shares
my blood to be left
by you to rot above
the earth without
a proper burial?

If you cast him out,
mark my words,
you will be casting

out three more corpses,
for I would rather die
on his behalf than for
your brother's wife!

Mind your own business,
and leave me to mine,
for if you get in the way,
I swear to the gods you
will wish you had backed
down, like a coward, when
I'm done dealing with you!

ODYSSEUS *suddenly appears.*

CHORUS

Lord Odysseus,
you have come
just in time, if
you are here to
loosen this knot.

ODYSSEUS

What is it, men?
From far away,
I thought I heard
the sons of Atreus
shouting over this
brave man's corpse.

AGAMEMNON

And from close up,
Lord Odysseus, we
have been made
to endure this insolent
man's loud insults.

ODYSSEUS

> What did he say?
> I can empathize
> when a man reacts
> to harsh words
> with a sharp tongue.

AGAMEMNON

> He heard harsh words
> because of his behavior.

ODYSSEUS

> And what did he do
> to provoke your anger?

AGAMEMNON

> He refuses to allow
> this corpse to remain
> unburied, but plans
> to violate my orders
> and bury it anyway.

ODYSSEUS

> Sir. Will you accept
> advice from a friend?

AGAMEMNON

> Of course. You are
> my chief adviser
> and greatest friend
> among the Greeks.

ODYSSEUS

> Hear me out, then, as a friend.

Do not cast out
this corpse or
leave this man's
body to the birds,
for in your rage
you will commit
a violation of justice.

I say this as some-
one who was once
the greatest enemy
of this man, after
being awarded
the arms of Achilles,
but in spite of his
wish to do me harm,
I would not dishonor
him in his death by
denying that he was
the bravest warrior
among the Greeks
who came to Troy,
second to Achilles.

No, it would not
be right to strip him
of all honors now
that he is dead,
as you wouldn't be
dishonoring him, but
the divine laws that
forbid us from mis-
treating a noble man
after his death, even
if you hated him
when he was alive.

AGAMEMNON

Odysseus, are you for me
or are you against me,
and for this man?

ODYSSEUS

I hated him
when it was
honorable
to hate him.

AGAMEMNON

He tried to kill us.
Is it not honorable
to tread upon him
now that he is dead?

ODYSSEUS

Son of Atreus,
do not revel
in your power,
when you have
the upper hand.

AGAMEMNON

It is not easy
for a leader
to keep his
hands clean.

ODYSSEUS

Yes, but it should
not be difficult
to heed the advice
of a good friend.

AGAMEMNON

> A noble soldier
> always obeys
> his superiors.

ODYSSEUS

> A general wins
> victory when
> he surrenders
> to his friends.

AGAMEMNON

> Do you remember
> what kind of man
> you are defending?

ODYSSEUS

> He was my enemy,
> but he was also noble.

AGAMEMNON

> And you have respect
> for an enemy's corpse?

ODYSSEUS

> I am moved by
> admiration for
> his greatness,
> rather than by hatred
> for his smallness.

AGAMEMNON

> He was a man
> of many turns.

ODYSSEUS

>Many of our friends
>later become enemies.

AGAMEMNON

>But do you wish to praise
>these so-called friends?

ODYSSEUS

>I do not see friends
>and enemies as
>mutually exclusive.

AGAMEMNON

>You will show us
>to be cowards today.

ODYSSEUS

>No. I will show us
>to be fair and just.

AGAMEMNON (*loudly*)

>Are you advising
>me to allow this
>corpse to be buried?

ODYSSEUS (*louder*)

>Yes, I am, for I will
>one day die and hope
>my body will receive
>the same treatment!

AGAMEMNON

> I see now that every
> man works for himself.

ODYSSEUS

> Who else should
> a man work for?

AGAMEMNON

> Then this decision
> will rest on your
> shoulders, not mine.

ODYSSEUS

> Either way, you are
> doing a good thing.

AGAMEMNON

> Even if you had asked
> me for a greater favor,
> I would have given
> you what you wanted.

> But know this: whether he rots
> on top of the earth or beneath
> it, he will always be my enemy.

> > AGAMEMNON *turns, walks to the edge of the*
> > *dune, and—with his back to the crowd—*
> > *gestures casually toward* AJAX's *corpse.*

> You may do whatever
> you wish with his body.

> > > AGAMEMNON *exits.*

CHORUS

> You are a wise man,
> Odysseus, and whoever
> says otherwise clearly
> doesn't know what
> he's talking about.

ODYSSEUS

> Teucer.

> Once I was your enemy,
> now I am your friend.

> I would like to help
> you give this man
> a proper burial,
> the kind of funeral
> only afforded
> to the noblest
> of warriors.

TEUCER

> I must thank you,
> Odysseus, for what
> you have done; you
> have exceeded all
> expectations. You
> were this man's
> greatest enemy
> among the Greeks,
> but just now you
> stood beside him
> and would not allow
> him to be dishonored
> by the generals, now
> that he is dead. They

wanted to expose his
body to the elements
and disgrace his name
forever! For that, may
the father Zeus and
the avenging Furies
bring them to Justice,
destroying them
as they wished him
to be destroyed!

I am sorry,
son of Laertes,
but it would not
be right for you
to join us
in the burial
or help us lift
the body,
for we might
offend the dead.

If you were to send
others from the army,
who once were his
friends, that would
be fine with us.

I will take care of the rest.

Please know that I hold
you in the highest regards.

As far as I'm concerned,
you are a good man.

ODYSSEUS

> Well, I had hoped to help,
> but if you do not want
> to accept my help,
> I understand. I will
> accept your word and go.

> > > ODYSSEUS *abruptly exits.*

TEUCER

> Enough!

> Too much time has passed.
> Some of you dig a trench!
> Others boil water over a fire,
> to prepare the ritual bath!
> Still others, go to the tent
> and retrieve his armor!

> > TEUCER *kneels down to address* EURYSACES.

> Boy, stand beside me,
> touch your father
> tenderly and help me
> lift his body, the best
> that you can, but be
> careful, son, for black
> blood still gushes from
> his warm wounds.

> > TEUCER *rises—still holding the boy's hand—and,*
> > *choking back emotion, shouts for all to hear:*

> Let everyone who called
> him a friend step forward
> to help this man, who was
> excellent in all ways, for

while Ajax lived, there was
no better man in the world!

That is all I have to say.

CHORUS

Men can understand
many things after
seeing them, but
no man can predict
what will happen
to him in the future
until it has been seen.

SOPHOCLES'
PHILOCTETES

AN INTRODUCTION

After a reading of Sophocles' *Philoctetes* for members of the Warrior Transition Unit at Fort Stewart, Georgia, a soldier came forward and stood by the stage. His eyes were red and swollen, and his hands trembled. He was choking back emotion, barely hanging on. "For a while now," he said, "I have been separated from my unit, the guys I fought alongside downrange. Being separated from your unit is like being stripped of your humanity. I think Sophocles wrote these plays to bring soldiers together, to restore their humanity." He leaned closer and made a broad, sweeping gesture. "Without our humanity, none of *this* means anything."

When the Greeks declared war against the Trojans and launched a thousand ships, there was one man who knew the way: a combat veteran named Philoctetes. He led the fleet halfway to Troy, but the seas grew choppy and dark storm clouds began to gather on the horizon. They needed a place to dock their boats and wait for the winds to shift.

Philoctetes knew of a deserted island, Lemnos, where they could seek shelter. He led the Greeks there. And as he was the first man to step off his boat, he was also the first to enter the temple of the local river goddess Chryse. While he stood in front of her altar preparing to make sacrifices, the sacred snake of the river goddess slithered up and bit him on the back of his foot. It was a poisonous snake, and its venom coursed through his veins. He fell to the ground, clutching his sides, howling in pain, calling out for mercy. But no mercy came.

For three long days, Philoctetes writhed in the dirt, moaning and wailing as the wound suppurated and pus began to drain from his heel. The stench of the pus and the sounds of his howls wore away at his fellow soldiers, slowly eroding their compassion. They had a wounded warrior on their hands, with no medicine to help him, and they hadn't even reached the battlefield. His screams were destroying their morale.

On the third day, the storm finally passed and the winds shifted back in the right direction. While the Greeks all boarded their ships and prepared to sail, the generals—Agamemnon and Menelaus—held an executive session. They consulted with Odysseus, director of Greek intelligence, and asked him what they should do with the wounded Philoctetes. Odysseus said, "I know this is going to sound harsh. I know we were taught to never leave a man behind. But in order to accomplish the mission, we need to leave him on the island."* And so they did.

From the rocky shores of Lemnos, Philoctetes gazed out at the sea, heartsick, as his own men sailed away and left him for dead. For nine years, he lived in a cave, in complete isolation, never seeing another Greek or hearing his own language. He scavenged for herbs to dull the pain of his wound and hunted down birds and game with an invincible weapon, a bow bestowed upon him by the hero Heracles, without which he surely would have died. But believing he was suffering for a reason, Philoctetes willed himself to live until the day came when he would finally be rescued and healed.

---

* These lines are my invention, aimed at sharpening and framing the ethical conflict—the good of one versus the good of the many.

The Greeks had been waging a seemingly unwinnable war at Troy for those same nine years. When they'd first set sail, none believed the conflict would last so long. No one had gone home or seen his family. It had been one continuous deployment. The Greeks were desperate to sack the city, burn it to the ground, and return home to their families victorious. But there was no end in sight.

The generals held another executive session and—at Odysseus' suggestion—decided to send a covert unit into Troy under cover of night to capture the Trojan seer Helenus and bring him back to the Greek camp, where he was tortured until he finally foretold the future. "Until the Greeks return to the island of Lemnos," he said, "and bring Philoctetes and his invincible bow back to Troy, Troy will never fall."

Odysseus was immediately dispatched to Lemnos. Being no fool, he brought along a young officer, Neoptolemus, the son of the recently deceased Achilles, as a decoy. When the play begins, Odysseus and Neoptolemus—along with Neoptolemus' soldiers—have recently landed on the beaches of Lemnos and are searching for Philoctetes, hoping to find him before he finds them. Neoptolemus will soon be ordered by Odysseus to betray the wounded warrior by winning his trust and capturing his invincible weapon. Neoptolemus, the untested officer, whose name in ancient Greek means "new to war," will soon be tested.

At the center of Sophocles' *Philoctetes* is a scream—the harrowing sound of a man who has been stripped of his humanity and reduced to the state of an animal. At the center of the scream is a question. As audiences in military and medical settings throughout the world have responded to the play, one certainty has emerged. Through modern medicine and warfare, we have developed the ability to sustain the life and prolong the abandonment and misery of individuals like Philoctetes. Indeed, for every suffering Philoctetes there is a deserted island featuring its own unique sense of isolation. Despite our best intentions, we have managed to create a vast subclass of chronically ill people who are permanently stranded between wellness and illness, who will never be cured. In the face of their unknowable suffering, Sophocles' play challenges us to look within and answer the question at the center of the scream: *Will you stay?*

CHARACTERS

(in order of appearance)

ODYSSEUS: *the director of Greek intelligence*

NEOPTOLEMUS: *an untested officer, the son of Achilles*

CHORUS: *the soldiers of Neoptolemus, whom he inherited from Achilles*

PHILOCTETES: *a wounded warrior*

CAPTAIN: *an operative of Odysseus*

HERACLES: *the greatest of all Greek heroes, so great he became a god*

ODYSSEUS *and* NEOPTOLEMUS *stand on a*
beach—their weapons drawn—scanning the
cliffs for movement.

ODYSSEUS

> Here we are, Neoptolemus.
> The isle of Lemnos.
> A no-man's-land,
> surrounded by the sea.
>
> It was here that I stranded
> the Malian, exposed him
> like an unwanted baby, pus
> draining from the sacred snake-
> bite gnawing at his foot.
>
> Just following orders.
>
> I can still hear the howling,
> the gnashing of teeth,
> that kept us from pouring
> libations, the screams
> that pierced the stillness
> before the sacrifice.
>
> No more words.
> Now is not the time to talk.
> We must catch him
> before he catches us.
>
> Be a good boy.

Go find a cave
with two mouths,
where in winter
the sun shines
at both ends,
and during summer
a cool breeze
carries sleep.

You might find a stream
running downhill,
if it's still there.

NEOPTOLEMUS *scales the rocks.*

Do this quietly.
Report to me quickly.
I want to know whether
his home is the same as
I left it, or some other place.

Then I will tell you
the rest of the story!

NEOPTOLEMUS

That won't take long, Lord
Odysseus. I can see the cave.
It looks just like you said it would.

ODYSSEUS

Up there or down over here?
I can't see well from where I'm standing.

NEOPTOLEMUS

Over here.
No sound of footstep.
I hear nothing.

NEOPTOLEMUS *carefully enters the cave.*
ODYSSEUS *scales the rocks.*

ODYSSEUS

> Be careful.
> He might be asleep.

NEOPTOLEMUS

> There's a hovel.
> It's empty.
> No man inside.

ODYSSEUS

> Look for signs of life.

NEOPTOLEMUS

> A bed of matted leaves,
> fit for a camper.

ODYSSEUS

> What else?

NEOPTOLEMUS

> A makeshift cup
> whittled from wood,
> a circle of stones for a fire.

ODYSSEUS

> A poor man's treasure.
> It must be his.

NEOPTOLEMUS

> There's something else. (Ugh!)
> Rags caked with carrion, drying
> discharge from an open sore.

ODYSSEUS *enters the cave.*

ODYSSEUS

Clearly we've found it,
the place where he lives.

He must be close.

How far could a man walk
on a foot that is sick from the Fury?

He's hunting for food
or searching for herbs
to extinguish the fire
of his ancient affliction.

Send your man as a lookout
to keep him from ambushing me.

It's me he wants most,
more than anyone else.

NEOPTOLEMUS

Consider it done.
Is there anything else?
Just say the word.

ODYSSEUS

Prove your nobility,
son of Achilles,
not only your body's
nobility. Whatever
strange things
are said here today,
always remember
you came here with me.

NEOPTOLEMUS

> Sir, yes, sir.
> What are your orders?

ODYSSEUS

> Pull the wool
> over his eyes,
> seduce him
> with your words.

> When he asks who
> you are, say, "I am
> the son of Achilles."

> That much is true.
> No need to hide it.

> Then you should say
> you are sailing for home,
> deserting the army
> that begged you
> to come in the first
> place, their "only hope"
> of taking Troy. But
> when you arrived
> and asked for the arms
> of Achilles, they said
> you weren't worthy
> of such a birthright
> and dressed Odysseus
> in your father's suit.

> Ad-lib insults, the more the better.
> Pull no punches. I'll be fine.
> Worry about the Greeks instead,
> for if we fail to steal the bow, *you*
> will never triumph over Troy.

Only you can do this,
not I, nor anyone else.

Too young to swear
the oath to Helen's father,
you shipped out to sea alone,
owing nothing to anyone.

I cannot say the same.

If he should see me,
through the sight
of his bow, I'm already
dead, and you will be next.

A thief of invincible weapons
must be clever. I know
it's not your nature, boy,
to manipulate and scheme,
but the taste of victory
will cut the bitterness
of shame, a few hours
in exchange for a lifetime.

NEOPTOLEMUS

Son of Laertes, it hurts
to hear of things I hate
to do. It's just not in me
to lie, not in my blood,
not in my father's blood.

The man's only got one good foot.
Surely we can take him together.

They sent me to help
you, sir, but I would
rather die honestly
than win deceitfully.

ODYSSEUS

Your father was noble.

When I was your age, I said
all kinds of things, and always
backed my words with fists.

That was long ago.

Now I know the strongest
muscle is the tongue.

NEOPTOLEMUS

Are you still
asking me to lie?

ODYSSEUS (*losing patience*)

I'm *ordering* you to catch
Philoctetes in a trap.

NEOPTOLEMUS

Why should I trap him,
if I can persuade him?

ODYSSEUS

He won't be persuaded
or forced to do anything.

NEOPTOLEMUS

What's so special
about his strength?

ODYSSEUS

It's the arrows.
They never miss.

NEOPTOLEMUS

> Then how do I
> get near him?

ODYSSEUS

> I already told
> you. A trap.

NEOPTOLEMUS

> But aren't you
> ashamed of lying?

ODYSSEUS

> Not if the lie is
> our only salvation.

NEOPTOLEMUS

> How will I keep a straight
> face, saying these terrible things?

ODYSSEUS

> Remember what
> you stand to gain.

NEOPTOLEMUS

> But what do I gain
> if he comes to Troy?

ODYSSEUS

> The bow will bring
> the city to its knees.

NEOPTOLEMUS

> Am I the one
> who will do this?

ODYSSEUS

> Without you *and* the bow,
> Troy will never fall.

NEOPTOLEMUS

> In that case, it
> might be worth it.

ODYSSEUS

> Sure it is. You'd walk
> away with two prizes.

NEOPTOLEMUS

> Which ones? If I
> knew, I might act.

ODYSSEUS

> People would say you
> were clever *and* brave.

NEOPTOLEMUS

> Let the river run its course.
> I'll do it, shamelessly.

ODYSSEUS

> Do you remember
> your orders?

NEOPTOLEMUS

> Of course, now
> that I've agreed.

ODYSSEUS

> Stay here and wait for him.

I'll look for the lookout,
so as not to be seen,
and send him back
to the ship. If it takes
too long, he'll return
in the guise of a captain.

Beneath his words, what-
ever he may say, will lie
a message for you.

May Hermes the Trickster
guide us both, and Athena,
victory goddess, who
always bails me out.

> ODYSSEUS *vanishes behind a cluster of rocks.*
> *The* CHORUS *moves in from all directions.*

CHORUS

We are strangers
wandering with-
out a map around
this paranoid island,
wondering what
to say and what
to stifle when
confronted by
a suspicious man.

What are your orders?
We trust your judgment.

Zeus gave you the gift,
the ancient scepter.

Hold it in your hand.

NEOPTOLEMUS

> Scatter out bravely
> into the underbrush!
>
> Scout the location
> where he sleeps.
>
> Stand ready to help when
> the lame warrior returns.
>
> I'll give you a sign.

CHORUS

> Yes, but where's the camp?
> How far away is he traveling
> from? What if he, all of a sudden,
> ambushes us from behind?

NEOPTOLEMUS

> Over there.
> Two openings.
> One home, where
> he rests against rocks.

CHORUS

> But where is the wretched man now?

NEOPTOLEMUS

> Hunger drags
> his wounded foot,
> not far away from here.
>
> He's said to spend
> his days hunting
> with flying shafts,
> consumed by pain,

and no one here
to ease his suffering.

CHORUS

Poor man. I pity him:
isolated and alone,
no one to nurse him,
he talks to himself,
sharing his body
with a brutal disease.

How does he do it?

The gods work well
when men suffer
endlessly and die.

This noble man,
inferior to none
of the first families,
claims nothing
from his species,
but lives among
the spotted deer
and shaggy goats
with his incurable
affliction, starving
for human contact,
crying out to Echo,
Echo crying out to him.

NEOPTOLEMUS

I'm not surprised.

If I know the gods,
this divine pain
from savage Chryse,

nymph of Lemnos,
stranded him here
for a reason, until
the time when Troy
would fall, his bow
and arrows arrested
on this island.

CHORUS

Silence!

NEOPTOLEMUS

What is it?

CHORUS

A noise, the kind a man
makes clenching his teeth
in agony, over here, now
over there. It sounds just like
an animal, crawling on all fours.

There, I hear it clearly again,
a body in pain, a man in great
distress, reduced to howling.
But listen—

NEOPTOLEMUS

　　　　—Tell me!

CHORUS

He's not far away.

Instead of playing
the pipe, as most
shepherds do, he
trips and screams,

making music
with his moans.

Maybe he caught sight of the ship,
anchored in the secret cove.

I'm frightened of his wailing.

PHILOCTETES *jumps out from behind a rock and*
slowly approaches the men, his weapon drawn and
trained on NEOPTOLEMUS *and the* CHORUS.

PHILOCTETES

Strangers! Tell me who
you are, sailing ships
to a place without harbors
or men. To which country
and race do you belong?

Your clothes appear Greek,
closest to my heart, but
let me hear your voices
so I can be sure . . .

Don't go!

I know how it looks,
this savage state of nature.

I am wretched,
afflicted, and alone,
with no one to talk to.

I have no friends.

Please!

If you want to be my friends,
say something, anything, but
never leave a man hanging.

NEOPTOLEMUS

> Let me be the first to tell you,
> stranger, we're Greeks, since
> that is what you wish to know.

PHILOCTETES

> You have no idea how sweet
> your voice sounds to a man
> who hasn't spoken or been
> spoken to in so long . . .
>
> But what brings you here,
> on which wind did you sail?
> Answer so I might know you.

NEOPTOLEMUS

> I was born on Skyros.
> Now I'm sailing home.
>
> Some people call me
> son of Achilles,
> others Neoptolemus.
>
> That is all you need to know.

PHILOCTETES

> Son of Achilles, dearest of friends,
> I knew your grandfather, Lycomedes.
> He was so proud when you were born.
>
> What adventures led you to this place?
> From which land did you last set sail?

NEOPTOLEMUS

> I am sailing away from Troy.

PHILOCTETES

What? I don't understand.
You were far too young
for the first wave of ships.

NEOPTOLEMUS

Were you there?

PHILOCTETES

You don't know
who you are
looking at.

NEOPTOLEMUS

How can I recognize the face
of someone I've never seen?

PHILOCTETES

Perhaps you've heard my name
or the myth of my misfortunes?

NEOPTOLEMUS

I'm sorry. I don't know
what you're talking about.

PHILOCTETES

I am wretched, hated
by the gods, if men
don't know my story.
Those who discarded
my weak body now laugh
silently, while the disease
grows stronger each day.

My boy, I am Philoctetes,
the keeper of Heracles'
bow, whom the generals
and Odysseus abandoned.

They left me here to die
from a snakebite,
in tattered rags, sleeping
in a jagged cave, starving
without much food to eat.

I only wish the same for them.

Imagine my surprise
when I awoke, the tears
I shed, the sound of my
sadness. All of the ships
in the fleet had vanished.

Alone with my infection,
I knew only pain. Time
demanded that I scavenge
for food with this sacred
bow, which saved my life.
I would crawl through deep
mud on stiff knees, scraping
my rotten foot against rocks.
When water was scarce, I
survived by collecting ice.
I spent cold winter nights
without fire, but rubbing
stones together for their spark,
I saved myself from certain death.

So you see. I have everything
I need here in this cave, except
a cure for my endless affliction.

Listen, and I will tell you
about this island. Sailors know
not to approach its rough shores.
It is not a destination for men who
know its dangers. Occasionally,
those who chance to end up
here take pity on me with food
and clothing, but never, when I
have asked, offer to take me home.

Nine miserable years!

This is what they have done
to me, the Greek generals
and Odysseus. I only pray
the Olympian gods visit
them with equal suffering.

CHORUS

I pity you, son of Poeas!

NEOPTOLEMUS

And I know what you mean
about Odysseus and the sons
of Atreus. They are evil men.

PHILOCTETES

What have they done to you?

NEOPTOLEMUS

If I could kill them all, I would,
so that they might know Skyros
to be mother of the boldest men.

PHILOCTETES

Well said, my boy!

What is the source
of your great hatred?

NEOPTOLEMUS

I will be honest with you, sir,
as much as it hurts to feel
the shame to speak of it,
what happened when I sailed
to Troy, after my father's death.

PHILOCTETES

The son of Peleus is dead?

NEOPTOLEMUS

His life extinguished by no man,
mowed down by Apollo's arrow.

PHILOCTETES

A noble way to die. God
and man, both noble. I'm
sorry, I want to hear
more about your troubles,
but first I must swallow
this feeling of remorse.

NEOPTOLEMUS

There is already enough sadness
in your life, poor man, for you
to shoulder another man's grief.

PHILOCTETES

I suppose you are right.
Where were we?
What did they do to you?

NEOPTOLEMUS

Odysseus came for me,
unexpectedly, one day
on a beautiful ship,
saying sweet words,
such as: fate, destiny,
divine justice, necessity.

An oracle had foretold
after my father's death
that I alone would take
the Trojan towers.

I alone would do this.

We sailed straightaway.

I wanted to see his body
before they put it
in the ground.

I longed to gaze
at his face, and
the Promise
stayed with me,
singing softly
in my ears:

I would be the one to end the war.

Two days later we landed
on the beaches of Sigeum,
where I was surrounded
by soldiers swearing
they saw him, my father,
Achilles, standing there
before them, still alive.

Sadly, they were mistaken.

I wept over his lifeless body.

Naturally, I went to the generals
and asked for what was mine.

I can still hear their filthy words:

"Son of Achilles, feel free to take whatever
you like, anything at all, *except* for the arms.
They now belong to Odysseus, son of
    Laertes."

Tears burst from my eyes.
My heart filled with rage:
"How dare you give my
weapons to another man?"

And Odysseus, who was standing
nearby, turned to me and said:

"Yes, boy, they were given
to me for a reason. I was there.
I saved them. I saved him."

I savagely attacked him
with every insult I knew,
and seemed to strike a nerve
when—filled with rage—he said:

"We were there. You were not
where you were supposed to be!
Need I say more? You will never
return to Skyros with these arms."

I sailed for home, empty-handed,
robbed of what was rightfully
mine by the sons of Atreus,
and Odysseus. And so anyone
who hates them is dear to me!

CHORUS

> Mountain goddess,
> Rhea,
> Mother Earth,
> Cybele,
> Womb of god,
> I called out to you
> when they stripped him
> of his father's arms!

PHILOCTETES

> Strangers, I understand your pain.
> As you crossed the ocean, it only
> brought us closer. It is my pain now,
> for I know the actions of evil men.
>
> Did Ajax stand by and let it happen?
> I find that very hard to believe.

NEOPTOLEMUS

> He was no longer among the living.

PHILOCTETES

> Is he also among the dead?

NEOPTOLEMUS

> He no longer sees the light.

PHILOCTETES

> Only the good men die,
> while Odysseus and
> the sons of Atreus
> should, but never will.

NEOPTOLEMUS

> They pin medals to their chests
> and command the Argive army.

PHILOCTETES

> But what about my old friend Nestor?
> Surely he would have tried to stop them.

NEOPTOLEMUS

> After losing his son Antilochus,
> he also lost his will to live.

PHILOCTETES

> Where can one look
> when they are dead
> and Odysseus lives?

NEOPTOLEMUS

> He is a slippery man,
> but he will one day slip.

PHILOCTETES

> What about Patroclus,
> your father's dear friend?

NEOPTOLEMUS

> Dead.

PHILOCTETES

> How do you make
> sense of the gods?
> They somehow take
> pleasure in turning
> the worst men away

from Hades. Nobility,
righteousness, valor:
all meaningless words!

NEOPTOLEMUS

I try not to think about it.
In the future I will gaze at
Troy from my distant island
with weary eyes. (The cowards.)

Rocky Skyros will be enough for me,
my home, my refuge from memory.

> NEOPTOLEMUS *abruptly changes direction.*

And so we must return to the ship.
So long, son of Poeas, goodbye.
May the gods lift your affliction,
relieve your relentless suffering.

Let's go! While the wind remains.

PHILOCTETES

Are you leaving already?

NEOPTOLEMUS

We have to be ready
if we are going to sail.

> PHILOCTETES *drops to his knees.*

PHILOCTETES

Then on my knees
I beg you, powerless
and lame, do not leave
me here alone in this
condition. Take me
with you. I know

it is no small thing
to ask, but I ask
you all the same.
Please, do the noble
thing, like your father
would have done. Deliver
me to Oeta, my home,
and receive a great reward.

It will only take a day.

Put me wherever you like,
the bow, the stern, the hull.
I won't disturb your men.
In the name of Zeus, god
of beggars, do this for me.
Say you will! Or take me
to your home. It is not far
from there to Trachis and
the wide river Spercheius,
where I may see my father,
whom I fear no longer lives.

I sent so many messages,
asking him to come . . .

Either he is dead
or the messengers
hurried home,
paying me no mind.

I ask you again. Save me!
Take pity on me. Deliver
me instead of the message.

CHORUS (*cornering* NEOPTOLEMUS)

Pity this man,
who has endured

countless problems
I would wish upon
none of my friends!

If you feel contempt
for the generals, sir,
then convert their evil
into good. Take him
where he wants to go
upon your swift ship.
Escape the gods' wrath!

NEOPTOLEMUS (*loud enough for* PHILOCTETES
to hear)

Those are kind words,
but I wonder what you
will say when you've
heard enough of his cries?

CHORUS

You will never hear us
say anything else. Never!

NEOPTOLEMUS (*even more publicly*)

It would be embarrassing
to seem less compassionate
than my own men. If you agree,
then I say the ship will soon
carry him home. I cannot refuse.
May the gods grant us smooth
seas, wherever we should sail.

PHILOCTETES (*overwhelmed*)

Dearest friends,
I never believed
I'd see this day!

But how might I prove
my friendship to you?

Come with me, my boy,
and after I have shown
you my humble house,
I'll give you a lesson
in courage and survival.

The first thing you learn
is to embrace your pain!

PHILOCTETES *begins to lead* NEOPTOLEMUS
into his cave.

CHORUS

Wait.
I see a man,
some stranger.
Find out what
he has to say.

The CAPTAIN—*sent by* ODYSSEUS—*crests the cliff.*

CAPTAIN

Son of Achilles, I asked this sailor,
who was guarding your ship, where
I might find you, when I stumbled
upon him, accidentally, on the beach.
I am the captain of a vessel sailing
from Troy to grape-rich Peparethus.
When I heard that you were here,
I thought it only right to warn you
of the Argive plans, not just plans,
actions unfolding at this very moment.

NEOPTOLEMUS

I thank you, stranger,
for your kindness. Please
tell me of these actions,
as well as their plans.

CAPTAIN

Old Phoenix, your father's teacher,
and the sons of Theseus pursue you.

NEOPTOLEMUS

To bring me back
by words or force?

CAPTAIN

That's all I heard.

NEOPTOLEMUS

They come to please
the sons of Atreus.

CAPTAIN

They'll be here soon,
not in the future, now!

NEOPTOLEMUS

What held Odysseus back?
Is he afraid of something?

CAPTAIN

He was following another man.

NEOPTOLEMUS (*glancing at* PHILOCTETES)

And who was this man?

CAPTAIN

> It was . . . First, who is this?
> And keep your voice down.

NEOPTOLEMUS (*loud enough*)

> This, sir, is the famous Philoctetes.

CAPTAIN (*under his breath*)

> No more questions.
> It's time to go.
> Get out of here
> as soon as you can.

PHILOCTETES

> What did he just say to you?
> Why all the whispering?

NEOPTOLEMUS (*even louder*)

> I'm not exactly sure what he is saying,
> but whatever it is, he must say it loud
> enough for you and these men to hear!

CAPTAIN

> Son of Achilles, please don't
> speak so harshly against me,
> especially to the Argive army,
> from whom I make a living.
> I am only a poor man. Perhaps
> I should never have told you.

NEOPTOLEMUS

> I hate the Greek army.
> This man is my friend.
> And since you also

claim to be my friend,
tell us all that you know.

CAPTAIN

Be careful, boy.

NEOPTOLEMUS

I have been careful my entire life.

CAPTAIN

You will be responsible
for what I am about to say.

NEOPTOLEMUS

Fine. Out with it!

CAPTAIN (*pointing at* PHILOCTETES)

This is the wanted man.

Odysseus swore
an oath to either
talk him into
returning to Troy
or to capture him
and bring him back
against his will.

The entire army heard
him say this with no
lack of confidence.

NEOPTOLEMUS

I don't understand. Why
would they cast a man out
only to force his return?

What compels them to do
this . . . Some angry god?

CAPTAIN

There was a seer,
named Helenus.
He was the noble
son of King Priam.

One moonless night
he went for a walk
by himself, the fool.

Odysseus took him
by surprise, captured
him in the shadows.

He was paraded
through the camp,
a proud spoil of war.

They tortured him,
poor man, until he
foretold the future:

Unless the Greeks
brought Philoctetes
back from Lemnos,
they would never
take the city of Troy.

And when Odysseus
heard the prophecy,
he made a solemn
vow to do just that,
with words or force,
if he should resist.

And if he somehow
failed to win this prize,
and parade him through
the camps, he said that
anyone who so desired
could hack off his head.

PHILOCTETES (*overcome with rage*)

That man is a disease!

Did he really swear
to take me to the army?

CAPTAIN

I don't know anything more.
I must return to my ship.
May the gods protect you both!

> *The* CAPTAIN *disappears over the rocks.*

PHILOCTETES

Did he really think
that he could charm
me with sweet words?

After all this time?

I would sooner befriend
the thing I hate the most,
the snake that bit my foot,
turning me into an invalid,
than listen to that evil man.

But he will dare to say or do
anything he pleases. At least
we know he'll be here soon.

Let's go,
right away,

sail for open seas,
as far as we can
sail from him.
Forget sleep!
We'll work now
and sleep when
we are safe!

NEOPTOLEMUS

The wind is not right.
It blows against the prow.
We must wait until it shifts.

PHILOCTETES

The weather's always good
when sailing away from trouble.

NEOPTOLEMUS

Yes, but the wind blows
against their ships as well.

PHILOCTETES

The weather is never bad
for predators on the hunt.

NEOPTOLEMUS

All right. Take what
you need and we'll go.

PHILOCTETES

There are a few things,
but not many, inside.

NEOPTOLEMUS

> What could you possibly need
> that I don't have on my ship?

PHILOCTETES

> A special herb that dulls
> the pain of this wound.

NEOPTOLEMUS

> By all means, get it.
> Anything else?

PHILOCTETES

> Missing arrows
> I might have dropped,
> scattered in the dirt.

NEOPTOLEMUS

> Is that the bow,
> the famous one?

PHILOCTETES

> Yes. There is no other.
> It never leaves my hands.

NEOPTOLEMUS

> May I get a closer
> look at it? Could I
> hold it in my arms?

PHILOCTETES

> Only you deserve
> to do this, and anything
> else you should desire.

NEOPTOLEMUS

> I do desire it,
> but only if it
> is right. I'll let
> you decide
> if I am worthy.

PHILOCTETES

> Your words are full of reverence.
> And it is right for you alone, who
> gives me sunlight and the chance
> to see my homeland, Oeta, where
> at the feet of enemies Father raised
> me to hold my head erect. You alone
> I trust to handle it, and then return it.
> Your actions are as noble as
> this weapon, for it was won through
> kindness, and so you will be the only
> man to touch it with your fingers.

> PHILOCTETES *extends the bow to* NEOPTOLEMUS.
> *Both of them grip it tightly.*

NEOPTOLEMUS

> I am not sorry
> to have met you,
> my newest friend.
> More valuable than
> any material possession
> is your humanity.
> Please, go inside.

> NEOPTOLEMUS *tries to pull the bow loose,*
> *but* PHILOCTETES *snaps it back.*

PHILOCTETES

> I'll ask you to join me,
> as my illness demands
> you to stand alongside.

PHILOCTETES *leads* NEOPTOLEMUS *into his cave.*

CHORUS

> There is a story,
> I heard it long ago,
> about the man Ixion,
> who crept upon Hera's
> bed with evil intentions,
> late one starless evening.
>
> Zeus tied him to a deadly
> wheel and spun it hard.
>
> But there is no story
> I have ever heard
> that matches the cruel
> and meaningless fate
> of this harmless man
> who has done nothing
> to deserve his pain.
>
> I sometimes wonder
> how a man can listen
> to the breaking waves
> that pound the shores
> of this desolate island.
> What tears he must cry.
>
> But no one hears him
> moaning as the snakebite
> slowly consumes his foot.
>
> There is no one to sing
> him a lullaby, or heal

his wounds with herbs,
if he should start shaking.

Like a baby, but without
a nursing mother, he crawls
on all fours, the infection
spreading up his spine.

He did not plant seeds
on sacred soil, but shot
quick arrows with his bow,
hunting down wild game.

Nine years without wine
to drink, poor man, and only
stagnant pools of rain.

And now he meets this man,
who promises to return him
to the nymphs of Malis, and
the river Spercheius, where
Heracles became a blazing god
in the flames atop Mount Oeta.

> NEOPTOLEMUS *follows* PHILOCTETES
> *out of the cave.*
> PHILOCTETES *stops in his tracks.*

NEOPTOLEMUS

Why are you silent?
Why are you still?

PHILOCTETES

Ahhhhhhhhhhhhhh!

NEOPTOLEMUS

What's wrong?

PHILOCTETES

It's nothing.
Go ahead of me.

NEOPTOLEMUS

Is it the pain of your affliction?

PHILOCTETES

No. It's passing. See.
I'm already feeling better.
OH GODS!!!!!!!!

> PHILOCTETES *doubles over in pain.*

NEOPTOLEMUS

Why are you groaning to the gods?

PHILOCTETES

I am asking them to show some MERCY!
Ahhhhhhhhhhhhhhhhhh!

NEOPTOLEMUS

What's the matter?
Why won't you tell me?
You seem like you're in trouble.

PHILOCTETES

I wanted to keep the pain
to myself, but now
it cuts straight through me.
Do you understand?
It cuts straight through me.
I am being eaten alive.
There is no I, only it.

If you have a sword,
chop here. Take my foot.
I want it off, I want it off!

NEOPTOLEMUS

What is this pain
that all of a sudden
strikes so quickly?

PHILOCTETES

You know, my boy.

NEOPTOLEMUS

No. What is it?

PHILOCTETES

How could you know?
Ahhhhhhhhhhhhhhhhh!

NEOPTOLEMUS

I can't bear to look
at your condition.

PHILOCTETES

I know. It's terrible.
It is beyond words.
Please, take pity on me.

NEOPTOLEMUS

What do you want me to do?

PHILOCTETES

She comes when
I have wandered

too far. Eventually,
if I am still, she goes.
Do not abandon me!

NEOPTOLEMUS

You wretched man,
unlucky in all ways.
Should I hold you
in my arms—

PHILOCTETES

—No, no, not that.
The bow, take it,
as you asked just
now, and keep it
safe while I sleep,
until the pain also
sleeps beside me.
And if they come,
I beg you, my son,
do not let them take
it from you, or we
both shall die!

NEOPTOLEMUS

Do not be afraid,
but hand it to me.
I will care for it as
if it were my own.
No one will take it.

PHILOCTETES *hands him the bow.*

PHILOCTETES

There, it is in your hands.
Kiss it to avoid the curse
that brought this trouble
to me and the ones before.

NEOPTOLEMUS *kisses the bow.*

NEOPTOLEMUS

I pray that the gods
grant us safe passage,
wherever we are going.

PHILOCTETES (*in unbridled agony*)

Ahhhhhhhhhhhhhhhhh!
I have a sinking feeling,
your prayer will not
be honored by the gods,
for as we speak, blood
is oozing from the sore,
a dark red sign of evil
things to come. The pain
swells underneath my foot.
I feel it moving upward,
tightening my chest.
OH, I AM WRETCHED!
Don't go. Please. Don't go.
You understand. You know.
Ahhhhhhhhhh. Stay with me.
I wish they could feel this,
Odysseus and the generals.
DEATH! DEATH! DEATH!
Where are you? Why, after
all these years of calling,

have you not appeared?
My noble son, take my body,
scorch it on a raging fire,
as I once burned the owner
of the bow that you now hold.

Why the silence?
Say something.
Where have you gone?

NEOPTOLEMUS

Your pain is painful to observe.

PHILOCTETES

It comes as quickly as it goes.
Be brave. I beg you to stay.

NEOPTOLEMUS

Don't worry. We will stay.

PHILOCTETES

You will?

NEOPTOLEMUS

Without a doubt!

PHILOCTETES

It is not right to make
you swear an oath.

NEOPTOLEMUS

It is not right to leave
you here alone to die!

PHILOCTETES

> Hold your hand
> over your heart.

NEOPTOLEMUS

> I swear I will stay!

PHILOCTETES

> Look up!

NEOPTOLEMUS

> Where?

PHILOCTETES

> Up there!

NEOPTOLEMUS

> Why are you staring skyward,
> your eyes and mind both reeling?

PHILOCTETES

> Release me.
> Release me!

NEOPTOLEMUS

> Release you? Where?

PHILOCTETES

> Just release me!

NEOPTOLEMUS

> I will not do it.

PHILOCTETES

> If you touch me,
> you will kill me.

NEOPTOLEMUS (*thinking wishfully*)

> You are beginning
> to sound sane again.

PHILOCTETES

> Earth, swallow this body
> whole, receive me just as I am,
> for I can't stand it any . . . longer.

> > PHILOCTETES *passes out.*

NEOPTOLEMUS

> He seems to be falling asleep.
> Look. His head is nodding
> and cold sweat coats his skin.
> Let him rest as the dark blood
> drains from his wounded heel.

> > *The* CHORUS *kneels down and confirms that*
> > PHILOCTETES *is asleep.*

CHORUS

> O Sleep, unaware
> of suffering or pain,
> gentle Sleep, breathe
> bright white light upon
> his eyes and heal his foot.

> > *The* CHORUS *turns to* NEOPTOLEMUS, *abruptly*
> > *shifting direction.*

> Be careful where
> you stand, do not

let your mind be
clouded by sympathy
for this wretched man!

Why are you hesitating?

The moment is now.
Choose correctly
and victory is yours
with one quick shot!

NEOPTOLEMUS (*sarcastically, at first*)

Don't worry. He can't hear us.

It is true we need the bow,
but it is clear we need him, too.

He is the one the god demands
return to Troy on our swift ship.

You should be ashamed to speak
of actions you don't understand!

CHORUS

Before the sick one wakes,
do the thing you came to do!

The wind is strong.
He sleeps like a shade
in permanent Hades night,
paralyzed from head to foot.
Act now and speak later!

PHILOCTETES *rubs his eyes.*

NEOPTOLEMUS (*through his teeth*)

Try to keep it down.
His eyes are opening!

PHILOCTETES *gazes at* NEOPTOLEMUS *and is*
overcome by emotion.

PHILOCTETES

Never did I imagine
waking to find you still
here patiently waiting
for the suffering to end.

The light is beautiful
after sleep, especially
when friends are near.

I see that you *have* come to help.

The generals waited
less than a week before
they had enough of me.

But you are from a noble
family. You remained,
in spite of the smell
and the loud groaning.

Now that it seems she's
left me for a while, give
me a hand, help me stand
up, and we'll walk together.

PHILOCTETES *takes* NEOPTOLEMUS' *hand.*

The wind is right.
We shouldn't wait any longer!

NEOPTOLEMUS

I am happy to see you
breathing without pain.

I was convinced you were
dying in front of our eyes,
at least it seemed that way.

But now lift up your body,
or if you prefer, my men
will pick you up themselves.

We are not afraid of heavy lifting.

PHILOCTETES

Thank you. Now, please help me
up as you have pledged to do,
by yourself, in case the awful
smell repulses your men. Sharing
the ship will be difficult enough.

NEOPTOLEMUS

Put your weight right here,
and I will help you stand.

NEOPTOLEMUS *slowly helps* PHILOCTETES
to his feet.

PHILOCTETES

Don't worry. My body
still remembers how.

NEOPTOLEMUS (*to himself*)

What am I supposed to do now?

PHILOCTETES

What was that? Are you all right?

NEOPTOLEMUS

I don't know what to say.

PHILOCTETES

What's the matter?

NEOPTOLEMUS

Is this the way it has to be?

PHILOCTETES

Are you having second thoughts?
I know my illness is repugnant.

NEOPTOLEMUS

Everything is repugnant to a man
who contradicts his own nature.

PHILOCTETES

But you are acting
like your father,
showing compassion
to a noble man.

NEOPTOLEMUS

I will be called a traitor.

PHILOCTETES

Not for your actions,
but your words scare me.

NEOPTOLEMUS

What should I do?

If I speak or remain
silent, I am a criminal.

PHILOCTETES

It is clear this man
intends to sail alone!

NEOPTOLEMUS

> That's not it. If I take you
> with me, you will suffer more.

PHILOCTETES

> I don't understand.
> What are you trying to say?

NEOPTOLEMUS

> I am done hiding.
> All will be revealed.
> You must sail to Troy
> and serve the sons of Atreus.

PHILOCTETES

> What was that?

NEOPTOLEMUS

> There's more.
> Wait until
> you've heard,
> before you jump
> to conclusions.

PHILOCTETES

> What are you planning to do to me?

NEOPTOLEMUS

> Save you from imminent danger.
> Then, together, you and I will
> save the Greeks and conquer Troy.

PHILOCTETES

> That is your plan?

NEOPTOLEMUS

Necessity demands I do this.
Don't be angry when I tell you.

PHILOCTETES

What have you done?
I should never have trusted you.
Give me back the bow!

> PHILOCTETES *lunges for the bow, but*
> NEOPTOLEMUS *pulls it tight.*

NEOPTOLEMUS

I'm sorry. I can't do that.
I swore an oath to answer
those who are in command.

PHILOCTETES

You fire!
You horror!
You evil man!

Look me
in the eye
and say it!

You take my bow,
you take my life!

> PHILOCTETES *falls to his knees again.*

I beg you,
son of Achilles,
in the name
of your father
and the gods,
do not do it.

NEOPTOLEMUS *looks away.*

He won't talk
to me anymore.

He won't even look
in my direction.

You harbors!
You mountains!
You wild beasts!
Hear what the son
of Achilles has done!

Holding up his hand,
he solemnly swore
to bring me home,
but shamefully
stole the sacred
bow of Heracles.

He intends to parade me
in front of the Greeks
like some fallen warrior.

He does not understand
that I am nothing
but a wisp of smoke,
a human shell,
a decomposing corpse.

PHILOCTETES *crawls in front of* NEOPTOLEMUS.

You don't have to do this.

Even now it's not too late.

I am lost in your silence.

Crawling to my cave,
naked and exposed,
stripped of my weapon,

I most certainly will die.
Once a hunter, hunted
by the mountain beasts.

Will you change your mind?
If not, then may you also die!

The CHORUS *approaches* NEOPTOLEMUS.

CHORUS

What should we do?
We await your orders.

NEOPTOLEMUS

For some time now
I have pitied this man.

PHILOCTETES

Oh, yes. Pity me.
Show some mercy.

NEOPTOLEMUS

I should never have left Skyros.
That is where the trouble began.

PHILOCTETES

You are not a liar,
like those evil men
for whom you work.

Do the right thing.

Give me back the bow
and sail home to Skyros.

NEOPTOLEMUS (*wavering*)

What do you think, men?

ODYSSEUS *suddenly appears on a rock overhead.*

ODYSSEUS

I'll tell you what I think—
hand it over to me.

PHILOCTETES

Who is that? It sounds like Odysseus.

ODYSSEUS

Well done.
It is Odysseus
whom you now see.

PHILOCTETES

It's over. I am destroyed.
Sold to my worst enemy.

ODYSSEUS

Precisely.

PHILOCTETES *desperately reaches for the bow.*

PHILOCTETES

Give it back!
Quickly, boy,
let me have it!

ODYSSEUS

That will never happen,
even if he wished. You
will accompany the bow,
willingly or by force.

PHILOCTETES

These men will bring me by force?

ODYSSEUS

If you don't agree to come.

PHILOCTETES

Sacred Lemnos,
where Hephaestus
keeps his fire,
will protect me.

ODYSSEUS

Zeus, ruler of the entire cosmos,
decided these things long ago.

I only carry out his orders.

PHILOCTETES

Only a hateful man
hides behind the gods,
turning them into liars.

ODYSSEUS

They speak the truth.
It's time for us to go.

PHILOCTETES

And I say it is not.

ODYSSEUS

I beg to differ.
You have no choice.

PHILOCTETES

> I see my noble father
> bore me into slavery.

ODYSSEUS

> You are equal to the noble men
> with whom you'll soon take Troy.

PHILOCTETES

> Never! Even if
> I have to jump
> from this ridge.

> > PHILOCTETES *lurches toward the edge of the cliff.*

ODYSSEUS

> Easy there—easy . . .

PHILOCTETES

> Don't move or I will bloody
> my skull on the rocks below.

ODYSSEUS

> It's not for you to decide.
> Seize him!

> > *Two members of the* CHORUS *grab*
> > PHILOCTETES *and pull him back.*

PHILOCTETES

> Let go of my arms!

> You used this boy
> as a smoke screen
> for your deception.
> Loyal to the army,

he followed orders,
and now look at him.
His face says it all.

He hates himself
for what you've
made him do.

It was you who taught
him how to lie, you
who ruined him forever.

Where are you taking me?
I am nothing to you now.
I might as well be dead.

How will you make sacrifices
in the stench of my suffering?

How will you ever set sail
with my howling? Isn't that
why you left me here to die?

You will surely die for this,
if the gods are just. They are!
Why else would they send
you back for me, after nine
long years? O Lemnos!
Punish these men and
cure me of the infection!

ODYSSEUS

There are many things
I could say, but I will
limit myself to this:

If you are looking for
an honorable man,
there is no one better

than I. It is my nature
to always win, except
when it comes to you,
to whom I now defer.

Let go of his hands.
He will stay here.
There is no need
for him, now that
we have the weapon.
Teucer and I know
how to handle a bow.

> The CHORUS *releases* PHILOCTETES.

You are useless.

Enjoy Lemnos.

Let's go! Perhaps the generals
will give me this weapon
as a reward for taking Troy.

PHILOCTETES (*to* NEOPTOLEMUS)

Did you hear that?
He plans to appear
to the Argive army
waving my weapon.

ODYSSEUS

Do not speak to me.
I am already gone.

PHILOCTETES

Say something,
son of Achilles,
before you go.

ODYSSEUS (*to* NEOPTOLEMUS)

> Come with me, boy.
> That's a direct order!
> Stop looking at him or
> you will taint our fortune.

> > PHILOCTETES *turns to the* CHORUS.

PHILOCTETES

> Strangers, don't you have feelings?
> Will you abandon me, too?

CHORUS

> This boy is our leader.
> We follow his command.

NEOPTOLEMUS (*privately, to the* CHORUS)

> Odysseus will reprimand me,
> but I order you to stay while
> the sailors prepare the ship.
> Pray that the gods help
> this broken man recover.
> But stand ready to leave
> when you hear the call.

> > NEOPTOLEMUS *sprints up to* ODYSSEUS,
> > *and they disappear over the ridge.*

PHILOCTETES

> You hollow cave,
> burning/freezing
> with the seasons,
> I am destined now
> to starve within
> your hollow walls.

I call upon the birds
of prey, the ones
that were afraid—
come visit me
now that I am
out of arrows!

CHORUS

This is your fault.
You made a choice.
The god is not responsible.

PHILOCTETES

I am wretched,
bones fractured
by the affliction,
isolated, no friends
to help me hunt
without arrows.

I am the sucker
who was fooled
by the great liar.

I wish I could
see him burn.

CHORUS

This is your divine portion,
not the result of one man's lies.
Direct your curses elsewhere,
for we have stayed in friendship.

PHILOCTETES

On some distant shore,
overlooking the great gray

ocean, he sits laughing,
as he handles the bow
he stole from my hands.

Dear bow, I never meant
for you to leave my sight.
I have failed. The trickster
will pervert your purpose
and use you for evil ends.

CHORUS

A man may state his case,
but once he has spoken
he should not act spitefully.
The man whom you hate
was just following orders.

Men are dying every minute.
He served the greater good.

PHILOCTETES

You packs of wild-
eyed creatures
no longer hunted
from your homes
by my quick hands,
roam without fear
across this island.

Take your revenge
on my sick body,
gorge your mouths
with rotting flesh!

I am ready to die.

CHORUS

> By the gods, if you respect
> goodwill or friendship,
> listen to us! We are friends.
>
> It doesn't have to be this way.
> You can choose to save yourself.

PHILOCTETES

> Why do you remind me
> of the ancient affliction?
>
> Why have you good men
> done this evil thing to me?

CHORUS

> What do you mean?

PHILOCTETES

> You want to take me to Troy?

CHORUS

> Yes. That would be best.

PHILOCTETES

> Leave me alone!

CHORUS

> With pleasure.
>
> Come on, men,
> we must head
> back to the ship.

PHILOCTETES

> Don't go!

By Zeus,
I beg you
not to leave
me here alone.

Please!

CHORUS

What is it?

PHILOCTETES

Oh, my foot!
My poor foot!

Come back,
strangers,
come back!

CHORUS

Why do you contradict yourself?

PHILOCTETES

Do not blame a man
for what he says
in the grips of pain.

CHORUS

Come with us,
just as we ask.

PHILOCTETES

NEVER! Not even if Zeus
scorches me with lightning!
May the Greeks perish, those
who rejected this lame foot!

Strangers, one last wish.

CHORUS

What is it?

PHILOCTETES

A sword, an ax,
anything you have.

CHORUS

What violent act are you planning?

PHILOCTETES

I want to cut off
all my limbs,
then my head.

There's only
killing, killing
on my mind.

CHORUS

Why?

PHILOCTETES

To find my father.

CHORUS

Where?

PHILOCTETES

In Hades.
He no longer lives
under the sunlight.

Dearest city,
I would love to see
you one last time.

I was the one
who left your
sacred streams
to help the Greeks.

Now I am nothing.

> PHILOCTETES *recedes into his cave.*
> ODYSSEUS *and* NEOPTOLEMUS—*still holding*
> *the bow—appear on the rocks.*

CHORUS

We should have left long ago.

ODYSSEUS (*addressing the* CHORUS)

Would someone
mind telling me why
you are still here?

NEOPTOLEMUS

It was my doing, sir.

I told them to stay
to right the wrong.

ODYSSEUS

What did you do that was wrong?

NEOPTOLEMUS

I obeyed you and the generals.

ODYSSEUS

And you think that was a mistake?

NEOPTOLEMUS

I defeated a harmless man with lies.

ODYSSEUS

What man? I see no man here.
What are you plotting against me?

NEOPTOLEMUS

Nothing new, but for the son of Poeas—

ODYSSEUS

Why am I suddenly afraid of your words?

NEOPTOLEMUS

—from whom I stole this bow—

ODYSSEUS

Surely you're not giving it back to him?

NEOPTOLEMUS

I was wrong to take it from him.

ODYSSEUS

This is no time for joking.

NEOPTOLEMUS

Oh, I am quite serious.

ODYSSEUS

How is it right to return
the bow I helped you win?

NEOPTOLEMUS

It was despicable.
I want to make up
for what I've done.

ODYSSEUS

Clearly you're not afraid
of the entire Greek army?

NEOPTOLEMUS

Not with Justice on my side.

ODYSSEUS

You *should* be afraid.

NEOPTOLEMUS

Your threats mean nothing.

ODYSSEUS

Not when we stop waging
war against the Trojans
and turn our attention to you.

NEOPTOLEMUS

Whatever you say . . .

ODYSSEUS (*menacing*)

Do you see my hand
resting on my sword?

NEOPTOLEMUS (*unfazed*)

Do you see mine?

ODYSSEUS

Fine. Have it your way.

The generals will punish
your insubordination.

ODYSSEUS *charges off toward his ship.*

NEOPTOLEMUS (*shouting at his back*)

> Wisely done!
>
> I hope you show
> the same sense
> in the future!
> It will keep your
> feet out of trouble!

> PHILOCTETES *emerges from his cave.*

PHILOCTETES

> What is all the shouting for?
> What do you want from me?

NEOPTOLEMUS

> Listen to my message without fear.

PHILOCTETES

> That's what you said the first time.

NEOPTOLEMUS

> I have changed my mind.

PHILOCTETES

> When you stole my bow?

NEOPTOLEMUS

> I need to know your decision.
> Will you stay here and suffer?
> Or will you sail with us to victory?

PHILOCTETES

> Don't waste your words.

NEOPTOLEMUS

That's your decision?

PHILOCTETES

An understatement.

NEOPTOLEMUS

I wish you would reconsider.
But if you are not convinced,
then I will stop trying.

PHILOCTETES (*searingly*)

Why would I listen
to the boy who stole
my means of survival?

Why would I do that?

You are the shameful
son of a noble father.
I hope you die with
the rest of the Greeks!

NEOPTOLEMUS

Take back your curse,
and take back your weapon.

NEOPTOLEMUS *extends the bow to* PHILOCTETES.

PHILOCTETES

You are trying to trick me again.

NEOPTOLEMUS

I swear to the gods I'm not,
with Zeus as my witness.

PHILOCTETES

Those are nice words,
if they indeed are true.

NEOPTOLEMUS

Judge actions, not words!

Give me your hand.
Here is your weapon.

Just as NEOPTOLEMUS *hands* PHILOCTETES *the bow,*
ODYSSEUS *reappears on the rocks.*

ODYSSEUS

In the name
of the gods
and generals,
I command
you to drop
that weapon.

PHILOCTETES

I recognize that voice.

ODYSSEUS

You are going to Troy,
no matter what the son
of Achilles aims to do.

PHILOCTETES *takes aim at* ODYSSEUS.

PHILOCTETES

Not if this arrow hits its target.

NEOPTOLEMUS *desperately grabs*
PHILOCTETES' *hand.*

NEOPTOLEMUS

Please, by the gods, don't shoot!

PHILOCTETES

Dearest boy, let go of my hand.

NEOPTOLEMUS

I will not let go!

ODYSSEUS *vanishes.*

PHILOCTETES

Why did you stop
me from doing it?

NEOPTOLEMUS

It would have done
neither of us good.

PHILOCTETES

At least we know
the ranking officers
of the Greek army
are afraid to stand
behind their words!

NEOPTOLEMUS

You have the bow.
Are you still angry?

PHILOCTETES

You have proven,
once and for all,
that you are the son
of noble Achilles,

greatest among
the living, greatest
among the dead.

NEOPTOLEMUS

Thank you for speaking
so well of my father and me.

Now—hear me out—I have
one last question to ask you.

Each man is required to bear
the weight of his own fortune,
doled out by immortal gods.

But when a man insists, as you
have, on suffering self-inflicted
pain, why should anyone pity him?

You have grown savage,
and will not take advice
from any man. You hate
those few who have tried
to help you, calling them
enemies. Nevertheless,
I will tell you the truth
about your disease. I call
upon Zeus to witness
what I am about to say.

Know this.
Burn it into your mind.

You contracted
this infection
from a god, when
you approached
the temple of Chryse
and stumbled upon

the hidden serpent
who protects her walls.

Know this, as well:

You will never find
a cure for the snake-
bite until you return
with us to Troy and
meet with the sons
of Asclepius.

There—at long last—
the burden of your
illness will finally
be relieved, and together,
with your famous bow,
you and I will topple
the Trojan towers.

We have a prisoner,
Helenus, a powerful
seer who foresaw
all of these things.

He said that Troy
will fall this summer,
and wagers his life
against his words.

Now that you know,
you must agree.

Return with us to healing
hands, then finish the story.

Immortalize yourself at Troy.

PHILOCTETES

How can I dismiss his words?

And how will I endure their eyes,
especially the ones who hurt me?

I want to live in the house of Hades.

It is not the past that haunts me,
but the future, living among men.

What sort of humiliation will I suffer?

I worry for us both. You should not
return to Troy, and neither should I.
They stripped you of Achilles' arms.
And you want to fight by their side?
No, it is time for us to go home.
Forget those evil men. Let them die.
You are not like them. Neither am I.

NEOPTOLEMUS

You have said many sensible things.
Now put your trust in the gods
and sail away from this island.

PHILOCTETES

To the shores of Troy
with this wretched foot?

NEOPTOLEMUS

Sail to freedom
from your illness.

PHILOCTETES

Why are you giving
such terrible advice?

NEOPTOLEMUS

What's best for you
is best for me.

PHILOCTETES

Aren't you ashamed
to say such things?

NEOPTOLEMUS

Why should I be ashamed
of helping a good friend?

PHILOCTETES

Do you mean the generals,
or are you speaking of me?

NEOPTOLEMUS

You are my *only* friend.

PHILOCTETES

But you are handing
me over to enemies.

NEOPTOLEMUS

With all due respect,
show some humility
in your misfortunes.

PHILOCTETES

You are killing me
with your words.

NEOPTOLEMUS

No. You don't understand.

PHILOCTETES

Did you forget the men
who abandoned me here?

NEOPTOLEMUS

The same men
will heal you
if you return.

PHILOCTETES

Not if I must
return to Troy.

NEOPTOLEMUS

I give up. You are impossible!
It's time for me to stop talking.
You can go on living this way!

PHILOCTETES

Let me suffer what I must suffer!
Make good on your promise.
Take me home. Stop avoiding it.
And never mention Troy again.
I've heard enough of your words.

NEOPTOLEMUS

If that's what you
want, then let's go.

PHILOCTETES

You have said a noble thing.

NEOPTOLEMUS *props up* PHILOCTETES *and*
helps him down the rocks.

NEOPTOLEMUS

Walk with me.

PHILOCTETES

As best I can.

NEOPTOLEMUS

But how will I escape the army?

PHILOCTETES

Don't worry.

NEOPTOLEMUS

What if they invade my country?

PHILOCTETES

I'll be there—

NEOPTOLEMUS

How will you help?

PHILOCTETES

With the arrows of Heracles—

NEOPTOLEMUS

What do you mean?

PHILOCTETES

I will keep them from your shores.

NEOPTOLEMUS

I hope you are right.

They reach the beach.

Say goodbye.
Kiss the ground of Lemnos.

   PHILOCTETES *kneels and kisses the sand.*
  HERACLES *suddenly appears high above them.*

HERACLES

Not until you hear
what I have come
to say, son of Poeas.

Your eyes recognize
the form of Heracles.
Your ears, his voice.

I left Mount Olympus
to reveal Zeus' desire:
Do not sail to Skyros,
but obey my command!

First I will remind you
of what happened to me,
the twelve labors
and how I won
glorious immortality.

You and I share
a common destiny.

Through suffering,
you, like me,
will achieve greatness.

When you accompany
this young man to Troy,
you will be released
from your awful affliction.

Then, with my bow, you will
bring down Paris, the man
for whom the war was fought.

You will sack
the city of Troy
and receive
the prize for valor,
carrying your spoils
to Oeta, the home of
your loving father.

Then you will burn the plunder
on a pyre in reverence to my bow.

I offer the same
advice to you,
son of Achilles,
for you are useless
without your friend,
he without you.

Protect each other like a pair of lions.

Remember,
when you conquer
Troy, the gods always
demand devotion.

PHILOCTETES (*overcome with emotion*)

You whose voice
I longed to hear,
you who finally
have appeared,
I will not disobey
your commands.

NEOPTOLEMUS

> I vow to do the same.

HERACLES

> Do not delay.
> The moment is now!
> The wind is right for sailing.

> > HERACLES *disappears.*

PHILOCTETES

> I call out to you who kept
> me company all these years!

> Farewell to the water nymphs!

> Farewell to the waves that beat
> against the cliffs and sprayed
> my head with salty brine!

> Farewell to Echo,
> and my rocky home!

> Farewell, mountain springs,
> and all of Lemnos
> surrounded by the sea!

> Give me your blessings for a safe
> voyage, wherever Fate is taking me!

CHORUS

> Let's sail with a prayer
> to the nymphs of the sea,
> that we may find our way home.

> > PHILOCTETES *and* NEOPTOLEMUS
> > *wade into the ocean, hand in hand.*

AESCHYLUS'
PROMETHEUS BOUND

AN INTRODUCTION

Prometheus Bound is an ancient play about a god who is imprisoned for stealing fire and giving it to man. Before the play begins, the trickster god Prometheus admits that he willfully committed a crime and is sentenced severely for his actions. He is placed in extreme isolation at the end of the earth for eternity. The play tells the story of how Prometheus came to be incarcerated, and how—through continued disobedience—he becomes the most iconic prisoner of all time.

During the War of the Titans, a brutal conflict between two opposing factions of immortals, Prometheus traded sides, turning on his own blood relatives, the Titans, and offering his services to the Olympians. Prometheus, whose name in Greek means "forethought," proved to be an excellent strategist for the other side, flawlessly predicting events before they happened. Zeus, who led the insurrection, called Prometheus his chief counselor, and, with his help, the Olympians won the war, locking the Titans away in the depths of the underworld for all time.

Shortly after Zeus came to power, he enacted a series of decrees that immediately caused Prometheus to regret his decision to collude with the enemy. Chief among these new edicts was the imminent extermination of the human race. Prometheus, who always possessed a special affinity for humans, could not conscionably stand by and watch this genocide unfold. And so, in an open act of political subversion, he gave fire to humans and taught them how to use it. From Prometheus' gift, these early humans derived many of the things that we now associate with what it means to be human, such as medicine and metallurgy, prophecy and storytelling, architecture and writing. Prometheus gave humans their humanity.

Prometheus Bound is not a courtroom drama. In spite of our natural inclination to sympathize with the protagonist, it does not concern itself with the justness of his civil disobedience or the fairness of Zeus' law. Instead, the play concerns itself with what happens to Prometheus once he is punished. Over the course of the play, he is visited by a number of characters. Each of them attempts to impart advice as to how he can lessen his sentence. But the longer his incarceration lasts, the more self-isolating Prometheus becomes. The more isolated he feels, the more compelled he is to kick, goad, threaten, taunt, and provoke his jailers until he is made by them to suffer. By suffering at their hands, Prometheus will achieve his objective, exposing the corruption of his captors and the injustice of his incarceration.

Prometheus spends the final moments of the play shaking his fists at the sky, rattling his cage, cursing Zeus, and deliberately inviting a far worse punishment than isolation. At the end of the play, he is buried, like his brothers, under a mountain of rock. And, as the story goes, when he finally sees the light of day, he endures the most horrifying form of torture ever devised. Every morning a giant eagle comes and gores out his liver with its fierce beak. Every night, his liver magically regenerates, only to be eaten again the next day.

Anyone who has visited a segregation unit in a maximum-security prison has seen a prisoner like Prometheus, who uses his body as a weapon against a system in which he finds himself, otherwise, completely powerless. Those who work in our nation's overpopulated corrections system encounter him every day. Many of these professionals also identify with Prometheus and his isolation. After performances of the play for prison staff—correction officers, social workers, and food-service workers—I have heard many audience members say, "I am Prometheus," relating the stigma, societal judgment, and loneliness associated with their profession to the character's solitary confinement. In listening to these audiences and hearing their unique perspectives, I have come to understand that anyone who sets foot in the criminal justice system has a stake in this story.

I first met Prometheus while touring the Jefferson City Correctional Center, a maximum-security prison in central Missouri. He was standing in the shower—rail thin, naked, soaking wet, and shivering. All I could make out in the dark recesses of the narrow cage that confined him were the whites of his eyes and the scruff of his patchy black beard. But as soon as he noticed the warden standing only five feet away, he leaned into the light, bringing his face up to the bars, and proceeded to make his case: He said he'd been deprived of food for seventeen days. All that time, the guards had brought him only beans. They knew he was allergic to beans and were trying to murder him, starve him to death and make it look as if he had refused to eat. He hadn't been allowed to shave or bathe, either. He had rights, he insisted. What about his rights?

The warden, a stoic man with small opaque eyes and a well-groomed handlebar mustache, listened to each of his complaints, then firmly replied: "Let me ask you this. Why did you get to take a shower today?" The prisoner stared blankly in his direction—momentarily struck silent by the line of inquiry—then launched into the same impassioned speech about the abuses he had been made to suffer, as if he simply needed to speak more forcefully to be understood.

When the prisoner was done with his monologue, the warden calmly answered his own question: "You got to take a shower because you ate something this morning. The more you eat, the more privileges you will get back." He steadily held the prisoner's gaze and nodded, as if to say: *This is how it works.*

The prisoner, who had just ended a hunger strike, and the warden, who spent most of his waking hours engaged in these types of negotiations, were locked in an age-old battle of wills, a struggle for power that could have been ripped from the pages of *Prometheus Bound.* The prisoner was fighting those in power with the only power he had left. By starving, he was trying to make a martyr of himself. By breaking down his own body, he hoped to break the will of the warden. Whatever he had done to be placed in solitary confinement was, at this point, irrelevant. All that mattered now was how he would leave it.

The word *marturos* in ancient Greek means "witness." A martyr is a witness. Prometheus was a god who broke the law. For this crime, he was locked away in solitary confinement, a punishment to which the United States is currently consigning approximately twenty-five thousand of the more than two million American citizens who now live behind bars, one of the few first-world countries still deploying this outmoded, dehumanizing punishment for long durations and on such a large scale. It's as if Aeschylus, too, was saying: *This is how it works.*

Prometheus Bound is the story of how martyrs are made.

CHARACTERS

(in order of appearance)

KRATOS: *a guard whose name means "force"*

BIA: *a guard whose name means "power"*

PROMETHEUS: *a trickster god who willfully broke
the law*

HEPHAESTUS: *the god of blacksmiths*

CHORUS: *nymphs of the ocean*

OCEANUS: *a trusted old friend of Prometheus*

IO: *a troubled nymph*

HERMES: *the young deputy of Zeus*

The edge of a steep ravine at the end of the earth.

KRATOS *and* BIA *stand—like sentinels—on either side of* PROMETHEUS.
HEPHAESTUS *hangs back, reluctant to take part in what is about to happen.*

KRATOS

> At last,
> we have
> reached
> the end
> of the earth,
> the waste-
> land called
> Scythia,
> where no
> one ever
> steps.

> The silence is deafening.

> Hephaestus,
> you have been
> summoned
> by Zeus,
> ordered
> to nail this
> convicted
> criminal
> to the high

rock face;
shackle
his hands
and feet;
lock him
down with
unbreakable
chains, then
leave him
dangling,
exposed to
the elements.

He is the thief
who stole your
pride, the fire-
spark, the secret
source behind
your arts, and
gave it to man.

That was his crime.
This is his punishment.

He is sentenced
to serve out
his immortal
life in isolation,
in which time—
unbound—
he will learn
respect for
the Law
and lose all
love for that
weak species
called men.

HEPHAESTUS

Kratos and Bia,
Zeus would be
pleased, nothing
remains for you
to complete
his orders.

Your work here is done.

I am the one
who must
nail the god,
bound by blood,
to the side of
this weather-
worn ravine.

My hands hesitate.

But I must
force myself
to finish
the job
we came
here to do.

The words
of an angry
father must
always be
respected.

HEPHAESTUS *approaches* PROMETHEUS.

Oh you high-
minded, fore-
sighted son
of Themis,

the one
we called
counselor,
I must now
chain you
to this lonely
cliff against
my will.

Though you
may struggle,
you will
never break
these bonds
and will
remain here
in this god-
forsaken place,
against your
will, for the rest
of Time, where
you will never
hear another
voice nor
gaze upon
a face again.

Slowly scorched
in the harsh sun-
light, your once-
radiant skin will
char black and
you shall breathe
sweet relief when
Night finally comes,
enshrouding the sky

with her dark cloak
spattered with stars,
and then sigh again
when the bright Sun
returns to thaw away
the freeze at Dawn.

Minutes will seem
like hours, hours
like days, days like
years, as the un-
relenting torture
wears you down.

And no one
will come
to ease
your pain,
for the one
who will free
you is not
yet born.

This is what
you get for
your com-
passion.

You should
have known
better, should
have shown
submission
when you
enraged
the gods.

But you
could not

resist
sharing
our secrets,
bestowing
upon men
more than
they deserve.

So now
in return,
shackled
to this cliff,
nailed flush
to the stone,
unable to
sleep or
stretch out
your legs,
you will
cry out in
vain, begging
for an end
to the end-
less suffering.

Zeus will not be moved.
New power is always cold.

KRATOS

Come on.
Let's do this!

We've waited
long enough.

This is no
time to
go soft.

Look at him
and tell me
he does not
make your
stomach turn.

The gods all
hold him in
contempt and
so should you.

After all,
he stole
your fire
and gave
it to men.

HEPHAESTUS

The bonds
of family
and friend-
ship are as
unbreakable
as these chains.

KRATOS

I would
never
deny it.

But what
about you?

Are you
prepared
to ignore
your orders

and dis-
obey Zeus?

Are you
not afraid
of his
retribution?

HEPHAESTUS

Kratos
and Bia,
always
heartless,
always
ruthless.

KRATOS

This is no
time for
wailing or
wasting
words.

The god has been condemned.

HEPHAESTUS

I hate
my hands
for what
they must do.

KRATOS

Your hands
are as blameless
as your craft.

You are an
instrument
of divine
justice.

HEPHAESTUS

I wish
it had
fallen
to some-
one else
to do this
filthy job.

KRATOS

We all shoulder
the weight
of our service.

No one is free
except for Zeus.

HEPHAESTUS

I feel
the weight
of this work
bearing
down on me.

I cannot deny it.

KRATOS

Hurry it up.
Here are
the chains.

Do not let him
see you falter.

KRATOS *hands* HEPHAESTUS *the chains.*

HEPHAESTUS

There. Look.
See for your-
self, the braces
are now ready.

KRATOS

Pin back
his arms.

Pound
the nails
down
deep into
the rock
with full
force.

HEPHAESTUS

Fine.
The dirty
work will
soon be
done,
faster than
you think.

HEPHAESTUS *pounds the chains into*
the rock with a stake.

KRATOS

> You have
> to hit harder,
> leaving no
> room for
> the clever
> one to
> wiggle
> his way
> out, and
> somehow
> set him-
> self free.

> HEPHAESTUS *pounds harder.*
> PROMETHEUS *howls in agony.*

HEPHAESTUS

> His arm
> is stuck
> to the stone.

> It will not budge.

KRATOS

> Now nail
> the other
> one down;
> make sure
> it's secure,
> so the wise
> one will
> soon learn
> how foolish
> it was to defy
> the one in power.

HEPHAESTUS *pounds even harder.*
PROMETHEUS *wails.*

HEPHAESTUS

No one
can find
fault in
my work
but him.

KRATOS

Now drive
the un-
breakable
stake
straight
through his
rib cage in-
to the cliff.

HEPHAESTUS *hammers a stake through*
PROMETHEUS' *chest into the rock.*
PROMETHEUS *howls like a wounded animal.*

HEPHAESTUS

Prometheus,
I groan with
you, as if your
pain were mine.

KRATOS

Be careful
who you groan
for, or you
may end up

groaning
yourself.

HEPHAESTUS

How can you
witness his
pain and not
avert your eyes?

KRATOS

It is easy
to watch
him get
what he
deserves.

Do not
forget
to lock
the bar
around
his waist.

HEPHAESTUS

Yes. I know.

Enough with
your orders.

You do
your job!
I'll do mine!

KRATOS

It is my job
to give you
orders and

ensure the
orders are
carried out
correctly!

Go down
and clamp
his legs
together.

HEPHAESTUS *hammers the clamps down.*
PROMETHEUS *weeps, nearly broken.*

HEPHAESTUS

There.
All done.
See.
It did
not take
so long.

KRATOS

Hammer
the chains
down hard
and double-
check your
work, for
the inspector
has high
standards
and will
not tolerate
shoddy
crafts-
manship.

HEPHAESTUS

> You look
> just like
> you sound:
> a foul-
> mouthed
> thug!

KRATOS

> I may be
> headstrong
> and short-
> fused but
> you are weak
> in the knees,
> my friend!

> HEPHAESTUS *pounds a final stake into*
> PROMETHEUS.
> PROMETHEUS *convulses with pain,*
> *reduced to a silent scream.*

HEPHAESTUS

> We can go now.
> His body is bound.

> HEPHAESTUS *averts his eyes and walks away.*
> KRATOS *moves closer to* PROMETHEUS,
> *standing only inches from him.*

KRATOS (*to* PROMETHEUS)

> Go ahead.
>
> Disrespect
> the gods.

Steal their
gifts and
waste them
on your
little pets,
the mortal
ones that
you have
come to
lavish with
affection.

But let
me ask
you this:
Where are
they now,
when you
are here
suffering
on their
behalf?

Will they
ever be
able to
lift you
off this
cliff?

We called
you Pro-
metheus
because
you always
seemed to

see around
the bend.

But all
along,
you were
blindly
guessing,
stabbing
in the dark.

Now some-
one will
have to lead
you out of
the shadows,
groping like
a beggar
into the light.

> KRATOS *and* HEPHAESTUS *walk off.*
> PROMETHEUS *is utterly alone.*

PROMETHEUS

You bright
blue skies.

You gusts
of wind.

You river
waters
running
toward
the ocean,
then
smacking

like laughter
against
the shore.

Oh,
Mother
Earth,
who
cradles
us all.

I call out
to you,
and to
the all-
seeing
Sun.

Witness
how the gods
now cause
me to suffer,
inflicting
immeasurable
pain upon one
of their own!

Look upon
the tortures
I shall endure
over this end-
less sentence,
passed by
the newly
self-appointed
patriarch
of the gods,

the so-called
blessed ones!

Listen as
I groan
in misery,
then hear
me moan for
the misery
to come!

Who knows
how long
the suffering
will last,
and when
I will finally
be relieved?

What am
I thinking?

I know the answer.
I have always known.

There is no
hardship
on the road
ahead that
I will not
have seen
around
the bend.

I must carry
the weight
of my fate
with grace,
knowing

Necessity
is non-
negotiable.

But I can
not seem
to stop
myself
from
speaking
out or
holding
my tongue
about what
has happened
here to me.

I gave
forbidden
gifts to men,
and in return
I am locked
away to ache
in isolation.

I foraged
for fire,
holding it
in a hollow
stalk and
handed it
over to
humans,
so they could
teach them-
selves
to master

every craft
and harness
its power
to transform
the world.

That was my crime.
This is my punishment,
nailed to the edge
of a precipice,
wholly exposed
to the great expanse.

PROMETHEUS *smells the air.*

What is that sound
and scent floating
down the breeze?
Is it heavenly, human,
or a mixture of both?

Has someone come
to the end of the earth
to gaze upon my pain,
to witness the suffering
of an unlucky god
who has been chained
to a rock for inciting
the hatred of the new ruler
and his followers through
abiding love for humans?

What is that vibration,
like thousands of
hummingbirds
fanning their wings?

The CHORUS *of Oceanids suddenly appears,*
hovering above PROMETHEUS.

CHORUS

> Do not fear!
>
> We flew
> to this for-
> gotten rock
> as quickly
> as our wings
> would carry us.
>
> It took a while
> to persuade
> our master
> to allow
> us to come.
>
> The pounding
> sound of metal
> being beaten
> invaded our
> cave and awoke
> us to action.
>
> We took off
> right away
> and sailed
> through
> the sky on
> strong winds.

PROMETHEUS

> You children
> of the Ocean,
> who circles
> the Earth
> with ever-
> flowing

waters,
look at how
they chained
me down with
irons to this
lonely crag
where I shall
stand guard for
the rest of time
over this abyss.

CHORUS

I see, Pro-
metheus,
but tears
cloud my
eyes as
they fix
upon your
body, broken
with unbreak-
able chains,
shamefully
stretched
against this
stone.

For there
is a new
ruler on
Olympus,
who makes
up laws
without
due process,

abusing
his power
with criminal
intent to destroy
all those
who dare
oppose him.

PROMETHEUS

If only
he buried
me deep
in the earth,
far below
Hades,
keeper
of shades,
underneath
the underworld,
in the darkness
of Tartarus,
clamped
with tight
manacles
that cling
to the skin,
so no god
could ever
take pleasure
in watching
me suffer.

But, instead,
he left me
here dangling,

whipped
by the wind,
writhing
in agony,
to amuse
my enemies.

CHORUS

What sick,
sadistic god
would ever
take pleasure
in your pain?

Who among
the gods does
not share in
your sorrow
as if it were
his own,
except Zeus,
who will stop
at nothing
to crush
the Titans,
who sprang
from the Sky?

His reign
of terror
will not
end until
his hunger
for violence
has been
satisfied

or some-
one clever
conspires
against him
and seizes
the empire
by surprise.

PROMETHEUS

Though my
arms and legs
have been
disgracefully
chained with
unbreakable
bonds to this
desolate rock,
the day will
come when
our fearless
leader will
appeal for
assistance,
asking me
to disclose
to him how
he will be
overthrown,
and by whom.

He will not
ask nicely
or with gentle
persuasion.

And I will
neither tremble
at his threats
nor reveal
what I know
until he re-
moves these
shackles and
offers me just
compensation
for wrongful
imprisonment!

CHORUS

You are brave
to say these things,
emboldened by
the pain, but you
should watch
your words, for
an all-consuming
fear pierces my
heart as I stop
to contemplate
your condition.

You may never
find relief from
this endless
persecution,
for the son
of Chronos
is merciless
and will not
be moved.

PROMETHEUS

I know he
is harsh and
lives above
the law, but
one day
when his
defenses
are down
he will be
destroyed,
and then
he will
come to
this cliff,
where I
will be
waiting,
and extend
a hand
of friend-
ship to me.

CHORUS

Tell us the story,
hold nothing back.

On what charges
were you arrested,
arraigned, and so
harshly sentenced?

We want
to hear
your sworn
statement,

unless it
causes you
undue pain
to say it
aloud.

PROMETHEUS

It is painful
to speak but
also to remain
silent; either
way I lose.

At the time
when the gods
went to war,
some for Chronos,
others for Zeus,
I offered my
services to
the Titans,
children
of the Earth
and Sky.

But they did
not heed my
suggestions
and rejected
offers to
help them
with well-
wrought
strategies,
thinking in
arrogance

they could
force their
way straight
to victory.

On many
occasions,
Mother
Earth
whispered
the future
into my ear.

The war
would not
be won
through
force but
with clever
calculation.

This is what she said,
time and time again.

But my words
fell on deaf ears.

Left with
no better
choice,
I aligned
with my
mother
and got
behind
Zeus, who
accepted
my help,

calling me
counselor.

Together,
according
to plan,
we buried
our father
and all of
his brothers
and sisters
in the darkness
of Tartarus.

And this is my reward.
This is how the tyrant
pays back my service
and my sacrifice, with
misery and isolation.

It is a sickness
suffered by dictators
to mistrust friends.

But you asked
about the charges
and why I have
been dealt with
so severely.

Let me explain.

Within seconds
of ascending
to his father's
warm throne,
Zeus began
handing out
powers to
the ones

who stood
beside him.

But when it came
time to deal with
poor mortals, he
intended to erase
the race and start
all over again.

Only I dared
defend them,
standing him
down, holding
my ground.

I saved men
from total
annihilation,
from almost-
certain death,
and now I am
to endure
these terrible
tortures—painful
to feel, almost
worse to observe.

I treated men
with compassion
but was not thought
worthy enough to
receive it in return.

Instead, I will
be displayed
for all to see,
so ruthlessly

abused that
even Zeus
averts his eyes.

My punishment
is a disgrace
to the one who
punishes me.

CHORUS

Someone
with a heart
wrought from
iron or stone
would still
feel your
pain, as if
it were
his own.

It was a grave
mistake to come
here to see you
in this condition.

It is torturous
to witness
your torment.

PROMETHEUS

I know. I know.
I am a horrible
sight to see.

CHORUS (*slightly accusing*)

> Are you sure
> you've told
> us everything?

PROMETHEUS

> I distracted
> men from
> Death.

CHORUS

> And how did
> you cure them
> of this affliction?

PROMETHEUS

> I blinded them
> with hope.

CHORUS (*deeply troubled*)

> You have
> given them
> a great gift!

PROMETHEUS

> I also gave
> them fire.

CHORUS (*shocked*)

> You taught
> the short-
> lived mortals
> how to make
> flames?

PROMETHEUS

And from
the flames
will come
their crafts.

CHORUS

And this is why—

PROMETHEUS

I was sentenced
by Zeus
to suffer upon
this rock with-
out relief.

CHORUS

And when
will it end?

PROMETHEUS

When he
decides
I've had
enough.

CHORUS (*furious*)

It's hopeless!

That will
never happen.

Don't you
see what you
have done?

It is not for
me to say,
especially
when my
words will
only cause
you pain.

So let's drop it.

Instead,
you should
focus on
finding
a way off
this rock.

PROMETHEUS (*embittered*)

It must be so
easy for some-
one in your shoes,
with such a clean
record and nothing
to lose, to pass
judgment and
dispense advice
to a convict.

But let me be clear.
I broke the law.
Do you understand?
I made a choice.

I knew what I was doing.

I helped men
and I hurt my-

self, but never
in my wildest
dreams did I
imagine this
would be my
punishment,
alone on this
cliff, exposed
to the elements.

But do not waste
your time feeling
sorry for me.

Listen closely
and I will
tell you what
the future
holds and
where this
all will end.

Share this pain
with me, for as
you know, pain
tends to wander.

Someday, you
will be the one
writhing in pain.

CHORUS

I hear
you clearly,
Prometheus,
and only wish
to learn more

about your
ordeals and
how this
all happened.

OCEANUS *suddenly appears in the sky—*
riding an enormous eagle—and lands
only feet from PROMETHEUS.

OCEANUS

I have come
a long way,
Prometheus,
to visit you,
riding bare-
backed on
a fierce bird.

I came
to share
your pain,
bonded
by blood.

But in spite of
our family ties,
you will never
encounter some-
one who holds
you in more
esteem than I.

As you will
soon learn
I do not
waste words,
and you will

never find
a better friend
than Oceanus.

PROMETHEUS

Why have you come?
To see me suffering?

Where did
you find
the courage
to leave
behind your
home, your
caves carved
from sandstone
by cold streams
to visit this
landlocked
strip mine?

Perhaps you
have come
to witness
the crimes
that have been
perpetrated
against me?

Perhaps you
have come
to share in
the misery
by quietly
observing
my pain?

Then get a good look.

See how the new ruler
deals with old friends,
even the ones who
helped him ascend.

Take in
the sight
of my dis-
figured
carcass
splayed
out like
a piece
of raw
meat along
these rocks.

OCEANUS

I see, Prometheus,
and I understand
that the last thing
you want to hear
right now is advice.

It is hard
to counsel
a counselor.

But I came
to say this:

Know yourself.
Know your limits.

We have a new leader.

You must
change your

ways and show
submission
during these
violent times.

If you
continue
to spray
such
hurtful
words,
aimed
at the Father,
eventually,
they will
strike
their target
seated in
the sky.

And then,
I assure you,
your current
troubles
will seem
like child-
ish trifles.

Stop scowling,
poor prisoner.

Concentrate
on escaping
this awful
situation.

Maybe you
think I have

nothing to offer
but stale advice?

But your wounds
are self-inflicted.

You lashed
yourself with
whiplike
words as
you ran on
at the mouth,
Prometheus.

Show some humility.
Cease and desist!

You will only
add to your ever-
growing pile
of problems.

Allow me to guide
you out of this mess.

Stop throwing fits
and raging against
this new regime.

You will only
makes things
worse for your-
self, tightening
the chains, for
a brutal tyrant
crushes enemies
without pausing
to ask questions.

That is all I have to offer.
Take it or leave it.

I might just be able
to get you released,
if you can hold your
tongue long enough
for me to speak on
your behalf to those
now in power.

Do you hear me?
Enough with the insults.

Or do you not see
in all of your insight
that your words will
only be used against you
to lengthen your sentence?

PROMETHEUS

It must be nice
to wash your hands
of the very crime you
helped me commit,
an accomplice
who manages
to maintain
his innocence.

Leave me alone.
This is none
of your concern.

Say whatever
you wish to him,
but your words

will never penetrate
his unpliable mind.

Look after yourself,
or you, too, might end
up chained to a rock,
writhing in pain.

OCEANUS

You are far-
sighted when
it comes to
friends, and
nearsighted
when it comes
to yourself.

My assessment
of this situation
is grounded in
facts, not words.

Do not reject
my offer outright
on account of
my enthusiasm.

I know I can get
through to Zeus.

And I have no doubt
he will grant my
request to release
you from this rock
at the end of the earth.

PROMETHEUS

I am, and shall
always remain,
impressed by
your endless
enthusiasm.

I find it infectious.

But please do not
trouble yourself
over me, for
the trouble will
only end up
belonging to you,
if you are truly
willing to get
into trouble.

Keep your
voice down
and step out
of the fray.

Though I am
obviously in
pain, I do not
wish to infect
others with
this affliction.

Not when
I think of
my brother
Atlas, who
shoulders
the weight

of the world
in the west,
struggling
to hold
heaven
and earth
in his arms.

Or Typhon,
that fire-eyed
creature with
a hundred heads
from the Cilician
caves, who
revolted against
the ruler, waged
war with the gods,
bared his fangs
and roared with
awakening rage
as he skulked
murderously
toward Zeus,
and was leveled
by a lightning
bolt that burned
him back to ashes.

His limp body
now lies dormant
near the ocean
buried below
Mount Etna,
his loud mouth
finally silenced.

One day he
will awaken
and, just as
Hephaestus
sits on his perch
pounding magma
into metal, so too
will Typhon's
sleeping rage
explode from
the mountain,
spewing forth
rivers of fire
consuming
the countryside.

But you know
all of this and
do not need me
as your teacher.

Protect yourself
as best you can.

I will waste
away until
the day when
the ruler's
pride has been
depleted and,
at long last,
his anger
evaporates.

OCEANUS

Prometheus,
are you not

aware that
words have
the power
to cure the
affliction
of anger?

PROMETHEUS

Yes. If you apply
this medicine at
the right time
and do not try
to force a raging
spirit to rest.

OCEANUS

So tell me this:
What is wrong
with trusting
your instincts
and acting
decisively?

PROMETHEUS (*exasperated*)

I find it
impossible
to speak
to someone
so simple-
minded
about what
could go
wrong if

I followed
your advice.

OCEANUS (*resentfully*)

Then let
me wallow
in my own
stupidity,
if this is
what you
wish to
believe.

Sometimes
the wisest
thing to do
is to act
like a fool.

PROMETHEUS

This will be seen
as my mistake.

OCEANUS

Clearly you
wish to see
me go home.

I can hear it
in your voice.

PROMETHEUS

I am worried
your sympathy

will brand
you an enemy.

OCEANUS

Of whom?
The one
who just
took office,
freshly seated
on his throne
of power?

PROMETHEUS

Yes. Be careful
what you say,
or he might fix
his sight on you.

OCEANUS (*sarcastically*)

I will learn
from your
misfortune,
Prometheus.

PROMETHEUS

If you had
learned
anything
from me,
then you
would no
longer
be here.

Go! Now!

Get out
of this
place,
and never
let me
see you
again!

OCEANUS

Your strong desire
to see me leave
is only matched
by my wish to go.

I will pilot this bird
back home, where
he will surely be
pleased to rest his
knees in the stables.

OCEANUS *mounts his bird and flies away.*

CHORUS

I bellow on
your behalf,
Prometheus,
as tears streak
my face, for
this is the Law
under the new
ruler, used
to subdue
the older gods.

The ground
itself is sick

with sadness,
groaning
beneath
our feet for
the dignity
stripped from
you and your
brothers.

The waves
no longer
sound like
laughter as
they crash
against
the shore.

The black
depths of
Hades howl
bitterly below,
as cold rivers
nearly freezing
cry silently
over your
isolation.

PROMETHEUS

I ask you not
to interpret
my silence
as arrogance,
or the digging
in of heels.

My mind
is paralyzed

with painful
thoughts
of this im-
prisonment.

I distributed
gifts among
the gods,
dividing
them like fat
from a bone.

I have nothing
more to say.

You know
the story
all too well.

Think about
the conditions
in which men
were living.

They had barely
learned to crawl
when I taught
them how to think
for themselves.

I do not mean
to disrespect them.

I only wish to
explain what
compelled me
to help them.

They had eyes,
but did not see.

They had ears
but did not hear.

Instead, they
stumbled
around in
the dark,
grasping
at shadows,
as the shapes
around them
shifted, as
if living
in a dream.

They had
no purpose
or sense
of place,
until I taught
them to build
houses from
bricks that
were baked
in the sun,
and showed
them how to
work wood.

They lived
underground
in colonies,
like little ants
who burrow
through soil
to construct

labyrinths
in the dark.

They were
completely
unaware
of the cold
winter frost
or the bright
bloom of
first flowers
in spring, or
summer's
endless days.

They were
dislocated,
completely
confused
about who
they were
and where
they stood,
until I gave
them reason,
and revealed
the mystery
of how
the stars
constellate
in the heavens.

I gave them
the alphabet,
and inspired
them to string

letters together
into words.

I showed
them how
to yoke
together
seething
bulls and
saddle them
down with
burdens
until then
shouldered
by men.

I tamed and
trained horses
to pull carts—
the ultimate
luxury.

And I built boats
from bent wood
with canvas sails
that billowed in
the wind, so men
could move
smoothly across
the open seas.

Though I
thought up
all of these
things on
behalf of

humans, I can-
not seem
to think my
way out of
this situation.

CHORUS

It is shameful
to see you in
this condition.

You are
like a gifted
physician
whose mind
has slipped,
and who no
longer knows
how to treat
his own illness.

PROMETHEUS

I have only
scratched
the surface
of my crime.

Wait until
you hear
about all
of the crafts
I conceived
for men.

You might
be surprised.

You may
remember
how terribly
they suffered
whenever
they got sick,
how their
rotting teeth
would rattle
as their frail
bodies shook
from the heat
of fever.

They had
nothing
to defend
them from
the onslaught
of illness,
no soothing
treatment
to stop
swelling,
nothing to
be chewed,
or swallowed
that would
soothe their
aching joints
and relieve
their pain.

They died off in droves.

That is, until
I taught

them how
to crush up
plants and
treat their
diseases.

I gave them
the gift of
medicine;
it was the
greatest
gift they
had ever
received.

I schooled
them in
the mantic
arts, showed
them how
to see around
the bend
by reading
dreams and
learning
to discern
the hidden
symbols
behind
ecstatic
sounds,
as well as
the flight
patterns of
predatory
birds with

twisted talons,
so they knew
which ones
signified
good things
on the horizon
and which ones
forecast gloom
by observing
their lives,
their loves,
and their
altercations,
and by learning
to interpret
the insides
of entrails,
as well as
the subtle
shapes and
shades of
internal organs,
such as the
gallbladder,
the liver, and
the bloody
bone marrow
that finds favor
with the gods.

Once blind,
they now fore-
see the future
in the thick

smoke of
charred offerings.

I helped them
mine the earth
for iron, bronze,
silver, and gold,
and showed
them how
to mold metal.

I taught them
everything
they know.

All of
their arts
descended
from me.

I gave humans
their humanity.

CHORUS

You should
look after
yourself,
rather than
wasting all
your energy
in service
of humans.

Then, when you
finally walk free,
I have no doubt
you will be no

less powerful
than Zeus.

PROMETHEUS

No.

That is not
the way
it will be.

My fate
was spun,
measured,
and cut
long ago.

I will be
crushed,
ground
down, until
there is noth-
ing left
to grind.

The suffering
will never end.

And when
I have been
reduced
to a shell of
my former self,
I will finally
be released.

There is no way
to outsmart Necessity.

CHORUS

> Who controls
> Necessity?

PROMETHEUS

> The Furies
> and the Fates.

CHORUS

> Do they hold
> more power
> than Zeus?

PROMETHEUS

> Even he can-
> not evade them.

CHORUS

> And what do
> they have in
> store for him?

PROMETHEUS

> I'll say nothing
> more; neither
> should you.

CHORUS

> Oh. Come now.
> Tell us. How
> bad could it be?

PROMETHEUS

Change the subject.

This is no time
for talking about
what is to come.

I must hold on
to the secret
with all of
my strength.

It's all I have left
to one day leverage
my freedom from
this miserable prison.

CHORUS

I hope
Zeus,
who rules
over all
things,
never turns
in anger
against me.

And I hope
I never
offend
the gods,
by failing
to make
sacrifices
alongside
the Ocean,

or by saying
something
out of line.

May I always
be guided by
the impulse to
do right and
never stray
from the path.

It is good
to live out
prosperous
long years
filled with
joy and hope,
all the while
celebrating
the gift of
existence,
but I cringe
to see your pain
and bear witness
to your end-
less suffering,
brought upon
you by your
love of humans
and your head-
strong refusal
to bow your
head before
the new ruler.

A little fear goes a long way.

Tell me, Prometheus,
was it worth it? Where
are they now, when
you are in need of
someone to help you?

How could these
meek creatures
possibly be of
any assistance?

Do you not
see how they
stumble around,
as if sleepwalking
through a dream,
groping blindly
in the darkness, un-
able to apprehend
the true nature
of anything they see?

They are guileless,
and helpless, and
nothing they devise
will ever change
the course of history.

This is all obvious
to anyone who
observes you
in your current
condition,
Prometheus.

You have destroyed your own life.

There will be no more
wedding songs, like

the ones we sang when
you seduced my sister.

There will be only
lamentations on be-
half of your sadness.

10 *suddenly stumbles to the edge on all fours—*
half cow, half nymph.

10

Hello?
Hello?

To what
country
have I
come?

What kind
of people
would call
this place
home?

And who
is this poor
prisoner,
chained to
the side of
a mountain,
coming un-
hinged in
isolation?

What was
his crime?

Oh, where
have I

strayed,
driven off
course by
my over-
whelming
grief?

Ahhhhhheeeeeeee!

Here it comes!

The memory
burns like
the bite of
a horsefly.

I am haunted
by visions
of the hundred-
eyed herdsman.

The one who
sees all—
called Argos.

He tracks
me down
from hell
and back,
never letting
me out of
his sight.

His dead eyes
shift in every
direction as
he sweeps
the ground

with constant
surveillance.

There is nowhere
to go where he
will not see me.

There is no use
in running, but
I run all the same,
racked with
hunger and
with pain,
haunted and
hunted along-
side the ocean.

The shrieking
of his wax pipe
rattles my mind,
leaving behind
a constant buzzing
in my ears that never
allows me to sleep.

Where have I wandered?

Why has he
saddled me
down with
so much
suffering?

And what was
my offense,
for which I
am now being

terrorized
by the horse-
fly memories,
my body
burning
with bites?

Set me on fire!
Bury me alive!
Feed me to beasts!

But do not
torture me
with silent
judgment.

For that is far worse.

I have been
punished long
enough to know
there is nothing
left to learn
from wandering
the earth.

Teach me
something
useful, like
how to escape
this prison.

Listen to
the sounds
of a cow-
horned
virgin
in pain!

PROMETHEUS

That must
be the voice
of the daughter
of Inachus.

She is tormented
by memories,
like horseflies
gorging on the
flanks of a cow.

Mistakenly,
she enflamed
the passions
of Zeus,
making Hera
sick with
jealousy.

Now she
roams
the earth—
a lone
fugitive
running
for her life.

10

How do
you know
my father's
name?

Tell me.

And why
do you know

my story
so well?

We both
are in pain;
that much
I can see.

But what do
you know of
the invisible
horseflies,
stinging me
into a frenzy?

Ahhhheeeeee!

I jump and flail
and sprint and
shake; my belly
aches with hunger.

I have come
to this place
at the end
of the earth,
hunted down
by Hera like
an animal.

If you know
something, then
tell me when
this will end?

What awful
things await
me around
the bend?

Is there
a cure for
my affliction?

Will I always be ill?
Say something.

Commiserate
with another
victim, an un-
lucky female
fugitive who
wanders in
search of relief.

PROMETHEUS

I will tell you
everything you
wish to know.

I will not
speak to you
in riddles,
but plainly,
as a friend.

You see
Prometheus
before you,
the god
who gave
fire to men.

10

Oh, unlucky
Prometheus,
most humane

of the gods,
why are you
suffering here
on this rock?

PROMETHEUS

I had just stopped
pitying myself right
when you arrived.

IO

Then perhaps
you will grant
my request?

PROMETHEUS

Ask me again
and I will tell
you everything.

IO

Who nailed
you to this cliff?

PROMETHEUS

Zeus gave the orders.
Hephaestus obeyed them.

IO

And what law
did you break
to receive such
a sentence?

PROMETHEUS

>   I have already
>   told you enough.

IO

>   Tell me one
>   more thing:
>   When will
>   my suffering
>   come to an
>   end? When
>   will I stop
>   wandering?

PROMETHEUS

>   It is better
>   to remain
>   in the dark
>   than know
>   the answer.

IO

>   Please do
>   not protect
>   me from
>   the truth.

PROMETHEUS

>   I mean no
>   disrespect.

IO

>   Then why
>   hold back

from saying
everything?

PROMETHEUS

I could.

But I do not
wish to break
your spirits.

IO

There is nothing
left to break.

Tell me what
I wish to know

PROMETHEUS

Since you
still wish
to hear it,
I will say it.

Listen closely.

CHORUS

Not yet!

Before you
begin, allow
us to ask her
a question
or two,
and speak
further
about her
affliction

and how
she first
stumbled into
this mess.

We want to hear her
version of the story.

Then you can tell
her how it will end.

PROMETHEUS

I will leave
it up to you,
Io, whether
or not you
will grant
their request.

Sometimes
it can be
helpful to
share pain-
ful stories
with sym-
pathetic
audiences
who will
cry along-
side you.

10

I do not
know how
to reject
this request.

So you will
soon hear
in plain words
everything you
wish to know,
as painful as
it is to speak
of my dis-
figurement,
as shameful
as it is to talk
of the dark
storm clouds
that rained
ruin upon me,
leveling my life.

How at night
I was visited
in my bedroom
by seductive
dream visions
attempting to
tempt me with
smooth words:

"You lucky
girl. Why wait
to lose your
virginity,
when the king
of the gods
pursues you?"

Or:

"Go now, girl,
to the grassy
meadows of
Lerna where
your father's
flocks and
cattle graze,
so Zeus will
find some brief
relief from his
lust for you."

Every night
my mind
was invaded
by these
fever dreams.

Then one
day I found
the courage
to speak to my
father about
what I had seen.

He dispatched
men straight
away to Delphi
and Dodona
to learn what
he could do or
say that would
please the gods.

They returned
with messages

that made no
sense, strangely
constructed
sentences and
the kind of
gibberish one
comes to expect
from oracles.

But he heard some-
thing that caught
his attention and
took swift action
obeying his orders,
under the direct
threat of violence
upon our family.

He quickly kicked
me out of the house
and had me expelled
from my homeland.

It was as painful
a thing for him
to do as it was for
me to experience.

But he did it
all the same,
convinced by
oracles that
if he failed
to act, our
house would
be leveled
by lightning.

As soon as I left
my home behind,
my shape began
to shift, and
then my mind
began to slip.

I grew these
horns, which
you can see,
and was tortured
by horseflies
biting my back-
side, causing
me to jump
around and
kick the air,
stinging me
into a mad gallop
for the springs
of Lerna and
cool streams
of Cerchnea.

Everywhere
I looked I saw
the herdsman
with a hundred
eyes, the one
called Argos,
watching my
every step,
hunting me
down like
a wounded
animal that

tries to run
but never
escapes the
hunter's rage.

And even
though an
unexpected
death swooped
in and stole
away his life,
I still see him
lurking in
the shadows,
in my dreams,
and sometimes
in the corners
of my vision.

I am still
tortured by
horseflies.

And still
goaded by
the gods
to roam
the earth.

Now that you have
heard my version
of the story, tell me
bluntly, without
sugarcoating your
words, what is left
for me to endure.

There is nothing
worse than some-
one who knows
the truth but will
not say it plainly.

CHORUS

I never
imagined
I would hear
such a story.

I am shaken to the core.

It is un-
thinkable
what has
happened
to Io.

I shudder to look
upon the suffering
of this innocent girl.

PROMETHEUS

Consumed by your fear,
you shudder too soon.

Wait until you hear
the rest of the story.

CHORUS

By all means, speak
and teach us a lesson.

Those afflicted
always begin

to feel better
when they know
the full prognosis.

PROMETHEUS

Your first request
was granted right
away, when you
asked to hear her
version of the story.

Now listen closely
to the second part
and learn what Fate
has in store for this
girl, the indignities
she still has left to
suffer at Hera's hands.

And you, daughter
of Inachus, if you
take what I say
to heart, you just
might learn where
the road will end.

From here, turn
toward the spot
where the sun
always rises at
dawn and move
across the fields.

Soon you will see
the Scythian nomads,
who live high up in

stilted huts of woven
twigs and branches.

Be sure to keep your distance.

Do not approach
them, for they are
heavily armed with
long-range weapons.

Instead, hug the coast-
line, where the waves
can be heard pounding
the rocks. To your left
you will find the iron-
working Chalybes,
a mean-spirited people,
hostile to strangers.

Then you will come
to the river Hybristes.

Those who would cross
it live up to its name,
for it is tame until you
reach the Caucasus,
tallest of all mountains,
where the river bursts
forth from the highest
peak before plunging
down the other side.

You must scale
these summits
high in the clouds,
and move south-
ward until you find
the Amazons, who

hate all men and
will gladly show
you where to go.

Then you will travel
to the Cimmerian
Isthmus, where you
will bravely cross
the Maeotic trench,
a narrow channel
between a large lake
and the Black Sea.

Men will forever
be telling the story
of your crossing
and will even name
the strait after you.

Bosporus.

At long last,
you will leave
behind Europe
and finally
arrive in Asia.

PROMETHEUS *turns to the* CHORUS.

Do you now see
how the violence
of the tyrant
spreads evenly
among his people?

He wished to take
this mortal girl
to bed and make

her a woman, but
now she is saddled
with endless suffering,
sentenced to wander
for the rest of her life.

PROMETHEUS *addresses* IO *again.*

Young lady,
you have every
good reason
to loathe
the one who
pursued you,
for this has
only been
the prologue
to your tragedy.

IO

Ahhhhheeeeeee!

PROMETHEUS

You screech
and groan
and claw
at the dirt,
but I wonder
what you'll
do when you
have learned
more about
the horrors
that await you.

CHORUS

Are you saying
she still has
more to suffer?

PROMETHEUS

A turbulent sea
of agonizing pain.

IO

What good am I alive?

Why not throw
myself over this
rocky ravine?

My troubles would
be over as soon as
I hit the ground.

It is better to die
young than to live
out a protracted death
over countless years.

PROMETHEUS

I suppose you
would not do
so well in my
shoes, since
death for me
is not an option.

No doubt it would
be a quick fix to
all of my problems.

For now I must
wait until Zeus
is stripped of
his powers for
my troubles to
come to an end.

IO

Will he ever fall?

PROMETHEUS

I imagine you
would be pleased
to see it happen.

IO

Of course.
He is the reason
I am in pain.

PROMETHEUS

Then you should
be pleased to know
that it will one
day happen.

IO

But who will take
the tyrant down?

PROMETHEUS

He will self-
destruct, a victim
of his own habits.

IO

And how will
he do this?

Tell me, if it
does no harm.

PROMETHEUS

He will marry
someone and
live to regret it.

IO

A goddess or
a woman?

Please say it
if you can.

PROMETHEUS

Why ask me this?
It is not to be spoken.

IO

Will his wife
be the one who
removes him
from power?

PROMETHEUS

She will bear
a son who will
become stronger
than his father.

IO

And is there
a way for him
to keep this
from happening?

PROMETHEUS

No, not unless
I am released
from this prison.

IO

But who would
release you
against his will?

PROMETHEUS

Only someone
from your line.

IO

What did you say?
An offspring of mine
will release you
from these chains?

PROMETHEUS

After thirteen
generations.

IO

Your prophecy
is beyond my
comprehension.

PROMETHEUS

Then do not try
to comprehend
all of the things
you must endure.

IO

Do not offer
me a gift, only
to take it away.

PROMETHEUS

I will only
offer you
one of
the stories.

IO

What are my
options? Lay
them out and
let me choose.

PROMETHEUS

Here is my offer.
I will either speak
about the suffering
that awaits you
around the bend,
or of the one who
will release me
from these chains.

CHORUS

> Please reveal one
> of these stories
> as a favor to her,
> and the other to me.
>
> Hold nothing back.
>
> Tell her about
> where she will
> wander, and tell
> me about the one
> who will spring
> you from prison.
>
> I am dying to know.

PROMETHEUS

> Since you are
> so obsessed
> with the truth,
> I will not
> refrain from
> telling you
> everything.
>
> First, Io,
> I will finish
> out the story
> of your sad
> wanderings,
> until it is
> burned into
> the backs of
> your eyelids.
>
> After you have
> crossed between

the continents,
walk eastward
toward the rising
sun, along the coast-
line battered by
waves, until you
arrive at Cisthene,
home to the three
daughters of Phorcys,
ancient maidens
who take the shape
of swans, sharing
one eye and only
one tooth among
them, they never
see the light of day,
nor gaze upon
the moon at night.

Close to them live
their three winged
sisters, the human-
hating snake-haired
Gorgons, upon whom
no man can look with-
out turning to stone.

Prepare for this
imminent danger,
and make sure to
avert your eyes.

Then be ready for
another unnerving
sight, the silent,
sharp-beaked hounds
of Zeus, called griffins,

and the cavalry of one-
eyed men, called
Arimaspians, who
live beside the River
of Abundance, known
for its ever-flowing
streams of gold.

Keep your distance
and you will eventually
come to a far-off land,
where a dark-skinned
people lives near
the springs from
which the sun rises
each morning and
where the Black
River runs its course.

Follow the river until
you find yourself
standing over a water-
fall, where the Nile
hurls its sacred stream
over the Byblian peaks.

The river will take you
to a three-corned land,
where, at long last, Io,
it has been decided that
you and your children
will found a distant
community on the other
side of the world.

If any of this remains
muddled to you or hard

to comprehend, ask me
whatever you like, as
I have nothing but time.

CHORUS

If there is anything
of her sad story left
to tell, please speak
now, but if you have
said everything, we
ask you now to grant
us our request, that
is, if it still lingers
in your memory.

PROMETHEUS

She has now heard
the entire story, but
just so she does not
dismiss what I have
said as the kind of
gibberish one comes
to expect from oracles,
I will account for all
of her ordeals to date,
to verify my story.

Rather than starting
at the beginning
of the myth, I will
focus on the events
that led you here.

You left behind
the Molossian fields
and reached Dodona

and the surrounding
region at the foot
of Mount Tmaros,
where the whispering
oaks, wonders of the
supernatural world,
addressed you plainly
in the rustling of their
leaves as the soon-to-be
famous wife of Zeus.

Sound familiar?

Tortured by horseflies
you madly galloped up
the shoreline until you
reached the Gulf of Rhea,
where you were repelled
by raging storms and
sent careening off course.

Rest assured that in
the future this section
of the ocean will be
called the Ionian Sea,
in homage of your
struggle to cross it.

Do you still doubt
my ability to look
beneath the surface
and see into the very
essence of things?

The rest of what
I have to say, as
I pick up the thread
of this unfolding

story, will be for
both of you to hear.

At the end of the earth
there is a city called
Canopus, where
the silt all collects at
the mouth of the Nile.

It is here where Zeus
will heal your mind
by stroking the side
of your face with
the palm of his hand,
and from this caress
you will bring forth
a baby named Epaphus,
who will seed the land
along the wide-flowing
waters of the Nile and
harvest all of its fruits.

Five generations later,
fifty young girls will
return to Argos, fleeing
against their will from
unnatural marriage to
their cousins, who, like
predators after prey,
will hunt them down,
swollen with passion.

Pelasgian Argos will
offer them asylum,
and, in the dead of
night, these women
will mount a surprise
attack against their

so-called husbands,
hacking away at them
with razor-sharp blades.

That is the kind
of marriage I
would only wish
upon my enemies.

But one of these
young women
will fall in love
with her captor
and spare her
husband's life,
preferring to be
called a coward
over a murderer.

She will give birth
to a long line of kings
who will rule Argos
for many generations
to come, and from these
countless men a hero
will descend, who will
be known throughout
the world for his
mastery of the bow.

He will be the one
to finally free me
from this prison.

This is the prophecy
that I heard fore-
told long ago by my
own mother, Themis.

To tell you the rest
would take too long,
and teach you little.

10

Ahhhhheeeeeee!

Once again
I am horse-
fly stung
into madness.

I cannot
stop shaking,
as an over-
whelming
fear invades
my mind.

My heart
rattles in-
side its
tiny cage.

My wild
eyes roll
back only
to reveal
the whites.

My feet again
begin to stray.

Strange sounds
come blurting
out of my mouth.

And my tongue
unleashes a steady

torrent of meaning-
less words in un-
controllable waves.

10 *gallops away—tormented by visions of gadflies.*

CHORUS

Words of wisdom
were once spoken
by the one who
uttered this warning:

Never marry up.

Workers with
well-worn hands
should not wish
to wed those
who have been
spoiled by wealth.

May Fate never
allow me to be
bedded by Zeus,
nor wedded to
another god,
for I cannot
bear to look
upon what has
happened to Io,
who wanders
the earth, an
enemy of Hera.

It is better to marry
on equal footing, as
far as I am concerned.

That way, there
is nothing to fear,
and no surprises.

I hope I never
catch the eye of
a lustful god,
though there is
no use in struggling
if it should happen.

Fighting only makes it worse.

It is impossible
to escape
the gathering
storm clouds of
Zeus' embrace.

PROMETHEUS

It is just
a matter
of time
before he
will be
brought to
his knees,
stripped of
his power,
a victim
of his own
obsessions,
thrown from
his throne,
the curse of
Chronos, his
fallen father,

ringing with-
in his ears.

All because
of a woman.

Not one of
the gods
will be able
to steer him
away from
destruction.

Only I know
the way out
of the woods.

Let him get
comfortable
lounging
in the clouds,
blithely
throwing
lightning,
as if it were
the answer
to everything.

It will not break his fall.

He is sowing
the seeds of
his own demise,
in spite of his
best intentions,
creating the
conditions
from which
an invincible

adversary will
one day arise
to silence his
thunder and
extinguish his
electrical fire.

And as he
plummets
to the earth
he will learn
the difference
between ruling
the universe and
being a slave.

CHORUS

Your words
can only
be wishes!

PROMETHEUS

What I wish is
what will happen.

CHORUS

It is hard
to imagine
Zeus will
ever answer
to another.

PROMETHEUS

The rope
round his

throat will
burn far
worse than
these chains.

CHORUS

Why are
you so
fearless
with your
speech?

PROMETHEUS

What is there
to fear if I
will never die?

CHORUS

He might
devise a way
to intensify
your pain.

PROMETHEUS

Let him
do what-
ever he
wishes!

I know
what is
coming
around
the bend.

CHORUS

Those who
lower their
eyes be-
fore un-
avoidable
disaster
are wise.

PROMETHEUS

Go ahead.

Cower.
Tremble.

Shake in
your boots
whenever
he enters
the room.

It does not
matter to me
what Zeus
decides to do.

Let him play
the part of
the king
for a while.

This much I know.
His reign will be short!

> HERMES *suddenly appears on the rocks below.*

HERMES

You there,
wise one,

embittered
prisoner,
convicted
criminal
who betrayed
the gods
by handing
our powers
over to short-
lived mortals.

Fire thief.
I speak to you!

Zeus
commands
you to name
the marriage
of which you
so arrogantly
have spoken,
the one that
will throw him
from his throne.

Do not clothe
your words
in the smoke
of twisted riddles,
but lay out
these events,
moment by
moment, in
exact order.

And do not force me
to return, Prometheus.

Zeus will not
be amused
by your in-
subordination.

PROMETHEUS

Boldly spoken,
and with a lot of heart,
especially for an assistant.

You are so young,
your power so new.

Like some petulant
adolescent you think
your house is made
of unbreakable boards.

But I have
seen the two
before him
plummet
from above,
just as I will
one day see
him plunge
from power,
quickly and
shamefully.

Did you somehow
suppose I would
cringe when you
came, shaking in
the presence of
a god still wet
behind the ears?

Then, I hate to be
the one to tell you,
son, nothing could be
further from the truth.

Run along, now.

Hurry back to the one
who sent you here, for
you will learn nothing
from questioning me.

HERMES

This is just the kind of talk
that got you into this mess.

PROMETHEUS

I would not trade
my present misery
for your slavery.

HERMES (*wryly*)

Better to be enslaved
to this rock in chains
than to serve Zeus
as a trusted messenger?

PROMETHEUS

It is a noble way to suffer
the insults of the insolent.

HERMES (*dismissively*)

> It seems to me
> you like to suffer.

PROMETHEUS

> I would like to see
> you up here trying it!

HERMES

> Why do you blame me
> for all your problems?

PROMETHEUS

> In short, I have no
> love for the gods
> who stole from me
> what I gave to them.

HERMES

> Your raving sounds
> deranged, as if you
> suffer slightly from an
> affliction of the mind.

PROMETHEUS

> Then let me be ill
> if my illness comes
> from loathing those
> who stranded me here.

HERMES

> You would be in-
> tolerable if you
> were not chained
> to this rock.

PROMETHEUS (*mocking* HERMES *with feigned raving*)

> Ahhhhhhhhhhh!

HERMES

> Unfortunately,
> the ruler has
> not learned
> this word.

PROMETHEUS

> Ever-unfolding
> Time will teach
> him the meaning.

HERMES

> You have learned noth-
> ing from suffering.

PROMETHEUS

> If I had learned
> anything, I would
> not be speaking
> to an assistant.

HERMES

> Obviously,
> you have
> no intention
> of answering
> my questions.

PROMETHEUS (*sarcastically*)

Come to think
of it, I do owe
Zeus a favor.

HERMES

You continue
to taunt me, as
if I were a child.

PROMETHEUS

Calling you
a child would
be insulting
to children.

You will never
learn anything
from these lips.

There is nothing
Zeus could do,
no torture device,
no isolation
chamber that
could extract
the truth from me,
until I am released
from the indignity
of this prison.

Let his rain of
lightning fire
come flashing
down upon my
head; let his
blinding white
ice storms and

earth-shaking
quakes blast me
from all sides,
freezing and
then shattering
this high rock
face, reducing
it all to rubble!

I will never tell
him how he will
fall from power.

HERMES

Think about how
you have done
so far, speaking
this way to him.

PROMETHEUS

These things were
all decided long ago.
I saw them coming
around the bend.

HERMES

Just relent,
you fool!

You have
proven
your point.

Now show
some humility
in the face of
your suffering!

PROMETHEUS

> You would sooner
> convince a wave
> not to crash upon
> the shore than get
> me to behave like
> some hysterical
> woman, waving
> my arms in the air
> with hands turned
> skyward, begging
> a bitter enemy to
> release me from these
> unbreakable chains!

HERMES

> I have spoken
> many words,
> but none of
> them have
> seemed to
> have reached
> your ears.

> I had hoped
> to convince
> you to change
> your course,
> to soften your
> approach and
> adjust your
> attitude.

> But instead,
> you struggle
> against me,

like a freshly
saddled colt,
taking the bit
between your
teeth and trying
to grind it down.

Thrashing about,
you seem to be
under the mistaken
impression that
intelligence is more
powerful than over-
whelming force.

But you are help-
less in your will-
ful obstinance.

If my words have
done nothing to
move you, then
I hope you will
begin to envision
the dark thunder-
heads kicking up
surf, spiraling
on the horizon,
before heading
in this direction
to rain torrents
of ruin upon
you from above.

First, Zeus
will assault
this cliff with

lightning shafts
until it crumbles
and your body
is buried deep
in the debris,
pinned beneath
the crushing
weight of broken
slabs of rock.

Then, after
a seemingly
interminable
period of time,
you will return
to the surface,
where a fierce
eagle will shred
your body with
its razor-sharp
talons, feasting
its voracious
beak upon your
liver until black
bile pools
at your feet.

Do not expect
the suffering
to ever come
to an end until
some god freely
appears and
volunteers to
take on your

troubles and
descend to
the black depths
of Tartarus on
your behalf.

Brace yourself.

This is the un-
adulterated truth.

Zeus does not know
how to lie, and he
will most certainly
bring all of these
words to fruition.

You had better
take a moment
to think it over,
and remember
that stubbornness
should always
be softened by
good advice.

CHORUS

Hermes' words
seem appropriate
to the present
moment, for he
asks you to set
aside your head-
strong behavior
in order to receive
his guidance.

Do as he says.

It is shameful
when the wise
continue to do
wrong even after
they have been
made aware of it.

PROMETHEUS

With his open-
throated howling,
he has told me
nothing that I did
not already know.

But there is also
nothing dis-
graceful about
enemies attacking
each other with
everything in
their arsenals.

So let the lightning
lash me from above;
let mighty thunder
rattle the heavens
and whip up the gales;
let a swirling storm
uproot the earth and
send giant waves
cresting skyward
into the orbits of
the stars and spheres;
let him pick up my

broken body and
cast it into the dark-
ness of Tartarus.

I will stand
in the eye
of the storm,
staring down
Necessity,
but my spirit
shall never
be broken.

HERMES (*to the* CHORUS)

These are
the thoughts
and words
of the insane.
Where in his
rambling rant
did he ever
sound grounded?

When will he come to his senses?

You who have
stood beside him
during this ordeal
should leave this
place immediately,
before the sound of
thunder stuns you,
stopping you in
your tracks.

CHORUS

Say something
else to persuade
us, for we will
never leave him
behind in order
to save ourselves.

We are willing
to suffer what
we must suffer,
for he has taught
us to hate traitors.

There is nothing
worse in this world.

HERMES

Then listen
to my warning,
burn it into your
memory, and do
not blame me
when the wave
of destruction
comes, or ever
let me hear you
say that Zeus
was responsible
for your suffering.

You will have
no one to blame
but yourselves,
for you will
have freely

elected this fate,
with full knowl-
edge of the con-
sequences.

HERMES *dives off the cliff and flies away.*

PROMETHEUS

The story now unfolds.

The earth shudders.

And up from its depths
rumbles the thunder.

The lightning fire
begins to flash.

The harsh winds
spin and twist,
kicking up dust.

And the down-
drafts clash,
gusting against
one another
in a funnel
cloud now
roaring toward
me, dredging up
dirt from the earth
and spraying it
into the sky.

It advances
deliberately
in this direction,
guided by the un-
seen hand of Zeus.

Oh, Mother!
Oh, Sacred Earth!

Oh, Heavenly Sky,
where the sunlight
always shines!

Witness the injustice
of my suffering!

PROMETHEUS *and the* CHORUS *are subsumed*
in thunder, darkness, and rock.

SOPHOCLES'
WOMEN OF TRACHIS

AN INTRODUCTION

A few years ago, I met a pathologist who knew as much about ancient Greek tragedy as he did rare diseases. When I asked how he came to read the classics, he told me that his mentor, a Nobel Prize–winning physician, required all his protégées at Columbia University to study Sophocles' plays, which he believed to be essential training for future physicians. Apparently, when he died, a slip of paper was found inside his otherwise empty wallet on which he had inscribed the last line of Sophocles' *Oedipus Rex,* "Count no man happy until he dies, free of pain at last," a fitting final lesson for his students.

What makes Sophocles' tragedies so relevant for doctors, patients, and caregivers today is his unsparing depiction of pain, suffering, mental illness, and the spiritual and existential anguish that accompany affliction. While it seems fitting that a pathologist would obsess over ancient plays that portray suffering and death, the direct connection between Sophocles' plays and Western medicine is anything but accidental.

These tragedies were written and first performed during the century in which the profession of medicine was formalized in the Western world; the Hippocratic oath— the bedrock of medical ethics in the West—was authored; and, according to Thucydides, a virulent plague wiped out approximately one-third of the Athenian population. Seen through this lens, and framed by decades of nonstop military conflict, it's clear that Sophocles' audiences would not have been strangers to the unadulterated agony portrayed in his plays, and, if the reactions of audiences today are any indication of how audiences may have responded nearly twenty-five hundred years ago, it is reasonable to assume that Athenians found relief in seeing their private struggles enacted onstage.

Sophocles' *Women of Trachis,* perhaps his most underappreciated and overlooked play, charts the outer limits of human suffering, in graphic detail, by depicting the death of Heracles, the greatest of all Greek heroes. The play begins with the ancient saying, strikingly similar to the last line of Sophocles' *Oedipus Rex,* suggesting that no man can assess the quality of his life until he is dead. The adage rings especially true for Heracles, whose life up until the play begins has been characterized by unprecedented accomplishments and unimaginable sorrow. As the son of Zeus and the mortal Alcmene, Heracles was born to blur the lines between human and divine, and destined to expand the boundaries of humanity itself, through his superhuman achievements and the extreme indignities he would inevitably suffer at the hand of Queen Hera, the jealous wife of Zeus.

Hera visited Heracles with madness, causing him to slaughter his own wife and children in a deranged, dissociative state, mistaking them for his enemies. As punishment for the murders, Heracles was sentenced by Apollo to serve as the slave of Eurystheus, king of Tiryns and Mycenae, who assigned him twelve famous labors, one more impossible than the next, such as slaying the fierce lion of Nemea, capturing the Erymanthian boar, and bringing back the three-headed hound—Cerberus—from the underworld. An oracle had foretold that if Heracles managed to complete all twelve of these labors, he would win everlasting fame and one day become immortal.

After miraculously completing all the labors, winning liberation from the king, and remarrying—this time, an enchanting beauty named Deianeira, who bore him several children, including a son—Heracles continued to pursue his destiny, through countless campaigns all over the world. For the fifteen months leading up to the start of the play, Heracles has been in Oechalia, Thessaly, waging war against yet another king, attempting to sack the city and return to his wife and children in Trachis. With each passing day, however, his wife's worries continue to intensify. Just before he departed, Heracles handed her "a tablet that predicted something terrible would happen if he took too long to return." Deianeira assumes the worst, but—as she soon learns over the course of a single day—the worst is unimaginable until it suddenly arrives with the relentless and savage cruelty of an ancient curse.

Women of Trachis has long been called a "problem play" by scholars, mostly for structural reasons, but people who have witnessed death or extreme suffering, or who have experienced it firsthand, have no problem making sense of the story. After a reading of scenes at Harvard Medical School, a senior oncologist stood up—his hands noticeably trembling—and remarked, "I have never questioned my views on euthanasia in more than thirty years of practicing medicine until tonight, when I heard the actor playing Heracles screaming." After another performance, a male hospice nurse, with long white hair and wearing a faded denim jacket, told an audience of doctors how sorry he was that they were not able to accompany their patients through death. "I see terrible things," he said, "but I also witness miracles every day."

As the hospice nurse aptly pointed out, Sophocles' *Women of Trachis* does not glorify death but rather challenges us to look closely at it and strive to find connections and meaning. In the play, dying heroically turns out to be Heracles' last labor, the one act that separates his mortal life from immortal myth. In the throes of immeasurable pain—more than any other man or woman could withstand—the hero begs his son to be his "doctor" by helping him to die in a fiery blaze atop Mount Oeta. This final scene explores the ethical and emotional complexity surrounding Heracles' request.

Though euthanasia was sometimes practiced during the fifth century BC, specifically in the form of mercy killings, the Hippocratic oath—the most influential medical treatise to survive from the ancient world—prohibits doctors from administering deadly drugs to their patients. For more than two millennia, its core principle—"do no harm"—has remained the ethical foundation of Western medicine, which aims to preserve life, almost at any cost. And yet Sophocles' *Women of Trachis* offers an alternative perspective, arguing that life should not always be preserved and that humans have an obligation to accompany the dying through death. When Heracles commands his son Hyllus to heal his body by setting it on fire, Hyllus wavers. If he is loyal to his father and his near-death requests, then he will betray himself.

We will all wade through these waters. Above all, we must attempt to remain loyal to ourselves. However, until we have come into contact with death, or the kind of unbearable suffering depicted in the play, it is hard to imagine how we might act. Sophocles' tragedies afford us the opportunity to rehearse for the inevitable and prepare ourselves to one day face it. "Count no man happy until he dies, free of pain at last."

CHARACTERS

(in order of appearance)

DEIANEIRA: *the middle-aged wife of Heracles*

NURSE: *her servant*

HYLLUS: *the teenage son of Heracles and Deianeira*

CHORUS: *local women from Trachis, servants of Deianeira*

MESSENGER: *an old man from Trachis*

LICHAS: *the messenger of Heracles*

CAPTIVE WOMEN: *war prizes from the city of Eurytus*

IOLE: *the young war bride of Heracles*

SOLDIERS: *Heracles' men*

HERACLES: *the greatest of all Greek heroes*

OLD MAN: *a local healer*

DEIANEIRA

> There is a saying.
>
> I've heard it spoken
> countless times
> by many old men.
>
> No one can know
> whether his life
> has amounted
> to anything or
> whether it was
> worth all the pain
> until he is dead.
>
> But I already
> know, without
> stepping foot
> in the world
> down below,
> the sum total
> of my suffering.
>
> I was born to live
> a miserable existence.
>
> When I was young,
> and still sleeping
> under my father's
> roof in Pleuron,

I was paralyzed by
an overwhelming
fear of marriage.

I had a stalker,
the river god
Achelous, who
appeared to my
father in three
mysterious forms
to ask for my hand:
a bellowing bull,
a venomous snake,
licking the air as
if twisting toward
a victim, and
a filthy old man
with the head
of a bull and
a beard of white
water cascading
from his face.

Whenever
I imagined
sharing his bed,
I curled up
on the floor
and prayed
for Death.

But then Heracles,
the beautiful son
of Alcmene and Zeus,
suddenly appeared
to free me from
the grips of the river

god sweeping
me downstream.

I averted my eyes
from the violence,
afraid I would die
on account of my
innocence, and can-
not say exactly what
happened that day.

But somehow,
thanks to Zeus,
god of contests,
Heracles won me
in the struggle
and I became his
bride, trading my
fear of marriage
for endless terror
of what might some-
day become of
the man I married.

We had children,
but like a farmer
who purchases
a piece of land
in a remote region
and only tends
to his fields in
certain seasons,
he spent most
of his time abroad
and hardly ever
saw them as they
were growing up.

For years, I patiently
awaited his return
and the triumphant day
he would be released
from his labors and his
slavery to the king,
who shall go unnamed.

When that day
finally came,
I was convinced
that all my worries
would at last be over,
but ever since he slew
the tyrant's mighty
son Iphitus, we have
been living on the run,
seeking shelter
in strange places
such as Trachis,
where we've been
staying with a friend
for some time.

It has been fifteen
months since
I last heard from
my husband,
the day on which
he left me, gasping
for breath, as searing
waves of pain burned
through my chest.

No one can tell me
where he is, or where

he has been, but some-
thing tells me he must
be suffering, for nothing
else can explain his
lack of communication.

He said as much
when he departed,
handing me a tablet
that predicted some-
thing terrible would
happen if he took
too long to return,
and so every day
I fall to my knees
and pray to the gods
that he will someday
come home safely.

NURSE

Pardon me, Deianeira,
for speaking out of turn,
but I feel it my duty
to make a suggestion.

On many occasions,
I have seen you
weeping over your
husband's long
absence, shedding
tears for him, as if
he were dead, but you
have a number of sons
who could be sent for
word of their father.

Why not send Hyllus,
who, no doubt, wishes
to know his father's fate?

He is coming this way,
walking swiftly from
the house in our direction.

If you like my suggestion,
then please make use of my
words, as well as your son.

HYLLUS *approaches the house.*

DEIANEIRA

Oh, my child, my son.

DEIANEIRA *rushes down the stairs to greet him.*

This woman is a slave
and from a low birth, but
she speaks with nobility.

HYLLUS

What did she say?
Please repeat it,
Mother, if you can.

DEIANEIRA

She said your father
has been gone for so
long that it would be
shameful for you not
to go search for him.

HYLLUS

I've heard only rumors
of where he might be.

DEIANEIRA

> What have you
> heard, my son?
>
> Where in the world
> is he rumored to be?

HYLLUS

> They say he's been
> enslaved all this time
> to a Lydian queen.

DEIANEIRA (*to* NURSE)

> If you believe that,
> you might just
> believe anything.

HYLLUS

> He has recently
> been released,
> I am told.

DEIANEIRA

> Is he alive or is he dead?

HYLLUS

> He is waging a new campaign
> in Euboea against Eurytus.

DEIANEIRA

> Did you know, Son,
> that he left me
> a prophecy about
> the city of Eurytus?

HYLLUS

No. What did it say?

DEIANEIRA

That he would either die
in this final act of war,
or triumph and live out
the rest of his life in peace.

He is standing on the edge,
peering over the precipice.

Won't you go and help
him now, for all will be lost
if he loses his life. But if he
is saved, then so are we!

HYLLUS

I'll go right away, Mother.
And if I had known earlier
about the things you just told
me, I would have gone to find
him months ago. But given
his reputation for overcoming
obstacles, even wrestling with
death and winning, it never
crossed my mind that he
wouldn't come home. But
now that I know the prophecy
and understand what it means,
I will search until I find him,
no matter what it takes, and
then return to tell the story.

HYLLUS *rushes toward the road.*

DEIANEIRA

> Go now, my son!
>
> Even if you are
> late to hear good
> news, the news
> will still be good
> for you to hear!

The CHORUS *congregates in front of the house to pray.*

CHORUS

> I call out to Helios,
> who combusts with-
> in the night at dawn,
> setting off a con-
> flagration that
> swallows the stars,
> only, at dusk, to be
> extinguished by
> night's cold cloak,
> shine your brightest
> light upon the son
> of Alcmene and Zeus.
>
> Show us, in your
> radiance, the way
> to where he lives:
> in the creeks that
> feed the Black Sea
> or perhaps buried
> in the narrow straights
> between land masses.
>
> Tell us, for nothing
> is invisible to your
> all-seeing eye,

taking in everything
in every direction.

The restless spirit
rattling within
Deianeira's chest
keeps her awake
at night, crying out
like a kingfisher
and staining her
face with an end-
less stream and
consumed by
fears triggered
by the silence
of an empty bed
and the long
absence of her
husband, Heracles.

As wave after wave
comes crashing against
the cliffs, whipped up
from the north or south
by an unrelenting wind
and sent barreling across
the open ocean, gathering
speed, churning, surging
toward the shore, so too
do the endless waves of
trouble come crashing
down upon Heracles,
but some god always
seems to help him keep
his head afloat, far above
the hidden depths of Hades.

So do not abandon hope
of his return, dear lady,
for the son of Kronos,
who rules the universe,
has ordered that mortals
live through cycles of
pleasure and pain, horror
and joy, anxiety and relief
over the long span of their
lives, like constellations
spinning in the night sky.

Nothing is permanent:
neither night nor
death nor prosperity
nor sorrow nor elation.

They are here one moment.
In an instant, they are gone.

You should take comfort
in this, dear queen, and
remember that Zeus always
looks out for his children.

DEIANEIRA

It appears you have come
because I am in pain, but
you will never understand
the severity of my suffering,
for you are blissfully
ignorant young innocents,
who will remain untouched
by the sun's damaging rays
or the unforgiving winds
and the bone-chilling rains,
until the night on which

you finally become women,
after which you will never
sleep through the night
again without waking up
and restlessly obsessing
over the health of your
husbands and children.

Only then, through the unimaginable agony of your
unknowable pain, will you
begin to understand mine.

There have been many reasons
for me to weep these past few
months, and there is yet another,
of which I just learned, that I
will now attempt to explain.

When Heracles set out on his
latest campaign, he left behind
an ancient tablet inscribed with
instructions for what we should
do in the event that he did not return.

In all the years
I've known him,
through countless
conflicts and trials,
he never once
mentioned Death,
but this time some-
thing was different;
he told me what
would be mine
and how he planned

to divide the rest
of the land among
his children. He
even prescribed
a time: if within
fifteen months he
did not return, he
would either be
dead or, having
somehow survived,
be free from pain.

He learned of this fate,
which he had been
granted by the gods,
from the priestesses
who preside over
the oracular oak.

Today is the day
on which it will
all be decided.

Unable to sleep,
I now live in fear
of losing the man
I love, the noblest
of all husbands.

CHORUS

Silence. I see a messenger
coming this way, an old man
wearing a crown of flowers.

The MESSENGER *appears at the foot of the steps.*

MESSENGER

> Queen Deianeira, I have come
> to free you from all fears!
>
> The son of Alcmene still lives.
>
> He has triumphed again in war
> and now returns with first spoils
> for sacrifice to the local gods.

DEIANEIRA

> What did you just say, sir?

MESSENGER

> Your husband will soon be home
> in a glorious show of strength.

DEIANEIRA

> And from what man have you
> learned this story? Tell me now.

MESSENGER

> From your husband's trusted
> messenger, Lichas, who just
> now told the story to a group
> gathered in the countryside.
>
> As soon as I heard,
> I came straightaway,
> so I would be the first
> to tell you and perhaps
> receive some small
> reward for my service.

DEIANEIRA

> But where is Heracles?
> Why hasn't he arrived?

MESSENGER

> He's in Malis,
> surrounded by
> crowds of people
> asking questions
> he feels he must
> answer, so he can
> learn something
> important in return.

> He's being held
> against his wishes,
> but, rest assured,
> you will see him
> again very soon.

DEIANEIRA

> I call out to Zeus,
> guardian of Mount Oeta,
> where meadows grow,
> untouched by man
> or the farmer's blade,
> you have finally made
> me a happy woman!

> DEIANEIRA *turns to the* CHORUS.

> Go now, spread
> the news through-
> out the house, like
> bright white rays
> of light at dawn!

CHORUS

> Swing wide
> the doors and

shake the mantels
with raucous cries
of celebration,
welcome home
the wandering
husband, Heracles,
and tell the men
to praise Apollo,
who protects us
all, with songs
of healing and
thanks. Call upon
his sister, from
Ortygia, the archer
Artemis, slayer
of deer, to raise up
torches made of pine
and rouse her nymphs
to dance the sacred
steps, as I do now,
in revelry, wreathing
my head with ivy
and whirling round
and round in bacchic
ecstasy, oh, oh, Paean!

Look, look, dear queen,
and see the radiant truth,
see it clearly, as it flashes
right before your eyes!

LICHAS *appears with a group of* CAPTIVE WOMEN.

DEIANEIRA

I see, dear women,
and I also see a strange

crowd coming this way,
led by my husband's
trusted messenger, Lichas,
who has finally arrived
and will be warmly
received if the news
he brings is welcome.

LICHAS

I am delighted
to finally reach
your home, where
I knew I would
be greeted warmly
when you heard
my news, which
is only fitting,
for a man should
always be treated
in accordance
with his actions.

DEIANEIRA *rushes to embrace* LICHAS.

DEIANEIRA

Dearest of men,
tell me first what
is foremost on my
mind. Is he alive?

LICHAS

When I left him,
he was certainly
alive, strong and
vigorous and un-
touched by illness.

DEIANEIRA

In his homeland
or a foreign place?

LICHAS

In Euboea, where
at the foot of Mount
Cenaeum he now
makes sacrifices
at Zeus' altars.

DEIANEIRA

Living up
to a promise,
or at the prompting
of a prophecy?

LICHAS

A pledge he made
to propitiate the gods
after leveling the homes
of the women now
standing before you.

DEIANEIRA *closely inspects the* CAPTIVE WOMEN,
who avert their eyes in fear.

DEIANEIRA

Who are they
and to whom
do they belong?

Their eyes demand
pity, if my eyes
don't deceive me.

LICHAS

> He hand-selected
> each of them,
> as personal prizes
> and first fruits for
> the gods, after sacking
> the city of Eurytus.

DEIANEIRA

> And has he been away
> all this time, waging
> war against this city?

LICHAS

> He has been held
> captive for most
> of this time by
> the Lydians, but
> do not be enraged,
> dear lady, for Zeus
> had a hand in his
> internment. Heracles
> was sold as a slave
> to Omphale and spent
> a year in the service
> of the barbarian queen,
> according to his own
> words. Overwhelmed
> with the shame of this
> indignity, he swore an
> oath to one day enslave
> the man who shackled
> him with chains, along
> with his entire family.

As soon as he had
cleansed himself
through acts of
ritual purification,
he marshaled an army
and marched upon
the city of Eurytus,
for this man alone
was the source
of his suffering.

Long ago, Heracles
had approached his
home, and Eurytus,
who had once been
his friend, assaulted
him with poisonous
words, bragging that
his sons surpassed
him in archery, even
though Heracles held
an invincible bow.

Later that evening,
drunk on wine,
he kicked Heracles
out of the house.

Boiling over
with insatiable
anger, Heracles
waited on the
cliffs of Tiryns
for Iphitus, who
went searching
for his horses

along the high
ridge trail,
absentmindedly
scanning for hoof-
prints in the dirt.

Heracles picked
him up and threw
him plummeting
over the edge
to his death.

And it was for this
that Father Zeus,
who sits on Olympus,
sold him into slavery,
as a punishment
for his treachery,
for if he had killed
Iphitus with his own
hands in a fair fight,
he would have been
forgiven, but the gods
do not look kindly
upon cold-blooded
acts of murder.

Heracles annihilated
the city of Eurytus,
enslaving the women
who stand before you
shattered, shaken,
and he exterminated
the men, silencing their
loud howls in Hades.

This was his command.

I followed him head-
first into the fight.

Your husband will
be here soon,
after he finishes
making sacrifices
to Zeus for allowing
him to sack the city.

That is the whole story.

I hope it pleases the queen.

CHORUS

You cannot hide
your happiness,
dear woman, for
what you just heard.

We can see it on your face.

DEIANEIRA

Why shouldn't I
be pleased to learn
of my husband's
imminent return?

I've suffered enough.

When he arrives,
I must meet and
exceed his elation,
jumping into his arms,
waving my hands
high in the air, all
the while remaining

careful not to revel
in his fortune for too
long, lest I provoke
the Fates and ensure
his swift destruction.

And yet, when I look
upon these miserable
women, homeless and
bereft of their fathers,
once free, now slaves
in a strange land, I am
suddenly overcome by
sympathy and sorrow.

Zeus, I sincerely hope
that I will never see
you turn against my
children in this way,
at least not while I am
still among the living.

Such are the thoughts
that race through my mind
as I gaze upon these girls.

DEIANEIRA *fixes her eyes on* IOLE, *the youngest and*
most beautiful of the CAPTIVE WOMEN.

Who is this one,
unhappiest of all?
What is your name,
dear? Do you have
a husband or a child?
You seem as if you
cannot understand
a thing I am saying,
but you also seem noble.

Tell me, Lichas, whom
am I addressing? Who
brought her into this
world and raised her?

For some strange reason,
she moves me the most.

LICHAS

Why ask me?
How would I know?
Maybe she's from
one of the noble
families in Eurytus.

DEIANEIRA

Did King Eurytus
have a daughter?
Is she of royal blood?

LICHAS

I have no idea.
I didn't pause
to ask questions.

DEIANEIRA

Didn't you learn
her name from
one of the others?

LICHAS

Absolutely not.
I completed
the mission
quickly, without
saying a word.

DEIANEIRA

> Tell me your name,
> dear girl, for it is wrong
> not to know who you are.

LICHAS

> I will be surprised
> if she speaks; for
> so far, ever since
> we left behind her
> homeland, the only
> sound she has made
> is violent sobbing.
>
> She hasn't yet learned
> to accept her fate, in
> spite of her misfortune.

DEIANEIRA

> Then I think it's best
> if we leave her alone
> and send her into
> the house, as I'm sure
> she wishes, so that we
> don't add to her pain.
>
> She has suffered enough.
>
> Let us all go inside, so
> that you may continue
> on your mission and I
> may ready the house
> for Heracles' return.

LICHAS *leads the* CAPTIVE WOMEN *into the house.*
The MESSENGER *approaches* DEIANEIRA.

MESSENGER

> Stay for just a minute,
> dear lady, so that you
> may learn, without
> Lichas being present,
> answers to your questions
> about the women you
> just welcomed into your
> home, answers that no
> one has been willing
> to tell you, which I
> have recently learned.

> Stay and all will be revealed.

DEIANEIRA

> What is it?
> Why are you
> trying to keep
> me from leaving?

MESSENGER

> Stand here and listen
> to what I have to say.
> As in the past, you
> will not find that I
> have wasted your time.

DEIANEIRA

> Should I call them all
> back to hear your words?

MESSENGER

> No. I wish to speak
> freely with you.

Let them stay
inside the house.

DEIANEIRA

We're alone. Please
tell me your story.

MESSENGER

Lichas is full of lies and
only speaks half-truths.

DEIANEIRA

What? I don't
understand. Tell
me plainly what's
on your mind!

MESSENGER

I heard Lichas
proclaim, before
a large crowd that
it was for this girl
alone that Heracles
leveled Eurytus,
stung by Eros, un-
done with passion
and completely
possessed, he
ravaged the city,
and tore down
the high towers
of Oechalia.

It wasn't because
of his yearlong

Lydian captivity
in service of
the queen for
murdering mighty
Iphitus, whom he
cast over the edge
of a cliff, screaming
all the way to his
untimely death,
though that is what
Lichas would like
you to believe.

When Heracles could
not convince the girl's
father to hand over his
daughter as a concubine
for a secret love affair,
he concocted charges,
marshaled an army,
and descended upon
the city to kill every-
thing and everyone
that breathed.

So you see, dear
woman, he did not
send her back as
a slave, not after
all that effort,
as she still arouses
his unfulfilled desire.

She is to be his bride.

I thought you had
a right to know

what I heard this
man say in Trachis
to a large group
of men, gathered
in the marketplace.

Ask any of them.

They will corroborate the story.

If what I just said
was painful for you
to hear, please know
that I have taken no
pleasure in saying it.

I have told you the truth.

DEIANEIRA

What has just happened?
What kind of trouble did
I just unwittingly invite
into my house? Does this
striking young girl not have
a name, as the man who
brought her here claimed?

MESSENGER

Her name is Iole,
daughter of Eurytus,
though he would
never know that,
since he never
bothered to ask.

CHORUS

I hate all criminals,
but those who

practice the art of
deceit are the ones
I hate the most.

DEIANEIRA

I am speechless.

Women, tell me
what I should do.

CHORUS

Interrogate the man,
and he may tell you
the truth, if you are
willing to use force.

DEIANEIRA

I will go and find
him now, for this
is good advice.

CHORUS

And what do you want
us to do while we wait?

DEIANEIRA

Stay right where you are,
since, without prompting,
this man is coming out
of the house on his own
and walking this way.

LICHAS *comes out of the house, ready to depart.*

LICHAS

> What would you like me
> to convey to Heracles, since
> I will soon be on my way?

DEIANEIRA

> Are you leaving already?
> You took so long to arrive.
>
> I would like to ask you
> a few questions about
> our recent conversation.

LICHAS

> If you have questions,
> I am at your disposal.

DEIANEIRA

> Will you speak candidly
> this time, so I will know
> whether to believe you?

LICHAS

> As Zeus as my witness,
> I will tell you all I know.

DEIANEIRA

> Who is the girl
> you just brought
> into my house?

LICHAS

> She is from Euboea.
> That is all I know.

I know nothing
about her parents.

The MESSENGER *steps toward* LICHAS.

MESSENGER

You there! To whom
do you think you
are now speaking?

LICHAS

Why are you asking
me this question?

MESSENGER

If you have any sense at all,
you will answer truthfully.

LICHAS

To my mistress, Deianeira,
daughter of Oeneus
and wife of Heracles.

MESSENGER

She is your mistress.
Is that what you said?

LICHAS

That's right.

MESSENGER

Tell me, then, how
should you be punished
if you are found to some-
how be deceiving her?

LICHAS

What do you mean,
"deceiving her"?

(*to* DEIANEIRA)

What is this man
trying to say?

MESSENGER

I am telling the truth,
something you seem
incapable of doing.

LICHAS

There is no
reason why
I should stay
and listen to
this insolence.
I will go.

LICHAS *makes a move,*
but the MESSENGER *blocks and corners him.*

MESSENGER

Not until you have
answered one
simple question.

LICHAS

Go ahead. Speak,
for you are clearly
not afraid to run
on at the mouth.

MESSENGER

> Do you know
> this woman
> whom you led
> into the house?

LICHAS

> Yes. Why do you ask?

MESSENGER

> Did you not say
> she was named
> Iole, daughter
> of Eurytus?

LICHAS

> When did I say that?
> And to what people?
> Who will testify that
> I said such a thing?

MESSENGER

> Hundreds of men
> from Trachis, who
> were gathered in
> the center of the city
> when you said it.

LICHAS

> Yes.
>
> I suppose I said some-
> thing about how I had
> heard these things, but

that is not the same as
reporting what you your-
self believe to be true.

MESSENGER

Did you believe your
own words when you
swore that she would
soon be Heracles' bride?

LICHAS

His bride? Who
is this stranger,
dear mistress?

MESSENGER

Someone who heard
you say that it was for
this girl that the city
was utterly destroyed,
and not enslavement
to the queen, but un-
requited lust for Iole.

LICHAS

Do not listen to this lunatic,
dear lady, but have him taken
away at once, for it is impossible
to reason with a man like this,
who spouts nothing but lies and
conspiracies as if they were true.

DEIANEIRA *steps close to* LICHAS, *meeting his eyes.*

DEIANEIRA

Swear before Zeus,
who strikes the heights
of Mount Oeta with
bright white lightning
that you will tell us
nothing but the truth,
for you will not be
speaking to a woman
who is unschooled
in the ways of men.

I am more than aware
of what happens when
husbands lose interest
in their wives, over time,
and what it means to be
discarded for another.

I only have the best of intentions.

I would never be
so foolish as to try
to fight with Eros,
for he is ancient
and powerful and
rules over the gods.

I am powerless before him,
and so is any other woman.

It would be insane
to blame my husband
for being afflicted by
this illness or
the girl, for that
matter, for infecting

him and my home
with her beauty,
bringing shame
upon our family.

No! No! No!
I must resist
the urge to
savage her
for stealing
my husband.

If he ordered
you to lie to me,
then you have
disgraced your-
self and your
profession, and
if you did it of
your own accord,
scheming about how
best to deceive
a faithful and
loving wife,
then you will be
called a criminal.

I demand that you
tell me the truth,
for it is beneath
a free man to lie.

Besides, I will know
if you stray from
your story, for
there are many

here who heard
you tell it before.

And do not let your
fears of what might
happen get in the way,
for it is not knowing
that will destroy me,
and there is nothing
you can tell me that
would surprise me,
for he has been with
many women before,
and never, in all this
time, has one of them
been assaulted by me
or slandered or slurred.

I would never harm
this girl, even if she
became the center
of his obsessions.

I felt sorry for her as
soon as I saw her; she
has been destroyed by
her own beauty and,
against her will, has
murdered her parents
and burned her home-
land to black ashes.

Let the truth gust forth
like a gale-force wind.

Save your lies for
someone who might
just believe them.

CHORUS (*to* LICHAS)

> Her words are
> honest and true.
> Do as she says
> and you will not
> live to regret it.

LICHAS

> Dear mistress,
> since you have
> shown your-
> self to be even-
> keeled and of
> sound mind,
> I will tell you
> the entire story
> and will hide
> nothing from
> you this time.

> Everything this
> man said is un-
> fortunately true.

> A sudden, violent
> lust overtook your
> husband as soon
> as he saw this girl,
> and it was on her
> behalf that the poor
> citizens of Oechalia
> were exterminated.

> He never ordered me
> to hide this from you.

I took it upon myself
to deceive you, fearing
that the truth would
cause you great pain.

It was wrong of me to do it,
especially if you feel I have
somehow done you wrong.

But now that you know
the entire story—out of
concern for you and your
husband—I ask that you
live up to your promise
and take pity on this girl,
for the strongest of men
has been, at last, defeated
by unbridled desire.

DEIANEIRA

I am still inclined
to show her kindness,
as I do not wish
to be infected with
this illness, or to wage
an unwinnable war
against the gods.

Come into the house,
so that I may give you
gifts for the gifts, which
you will carry to Heracles,
along with my message.

It would not be right for
you to leave without
receiving something in

return for all your efforts
after traveling all this way.

DEIANEIRA *leads* LICHAS, *the* MESSENGER,
and the NURSE *inside.*

CHORUS

Aphrodite
overpowers
her enemies
and always
emerges
victorious
in the end.

I will not talk
about other gods,
or how she eluded
Zeus, black Hades,
or Poseidon, who
shakes the earth.

Over the years,
many suitors
have vied for
Deianeira's hand.

First came
the river god
Achelous, who
appeared as
a long-horned
bull with thick
cloven hooves.

Then came
the son of Zeus,
with his club

and his in-
vincible bow,
all the way
from Thebes.

They bitterly
clashed over
who would
take her to bed,
as Aphrodite
stood on the side-
lines and judged
the struggle:
muscles were torn,
ligaments ripped,
horns broken,
bones snapped,
throats choked,
as they grunted
and butted fore-
heads, while she
waited patiently
on the ridge
to be thrown
over some-
one's shoulder
and taken away,
snatched up like
a calf that has
strayed from
the herd and
suddenly can't
see her mother.

DEIANEIRA *rushes out of the house, unseen—*
under her arm, a wooden box.

DEIANEIRA

Dear women,
while the men
are saying
their final
goodbyes
to the women
within, I slipped
outside, while
no one was
looking, to
speak with
you in private
about my un-
folding plans
and to elicit
your sympathy
for what I
have endured.

I invited
the innocent
princess into
my home,
whom I fear
no longer
so innocent,
now that my
husband has
had his way
with her, under

the covers, so
that the three
of us will soon
be sharing
a single bed.

This is the gift
that Heracles,
"the righteous
and dependable,"
brings me back
from battle for
waiting faithfully
for him to return.

Try as I may,
I cannot seem
to sustain my
rage against
him, not when
I imagine how
he was ravaged
by passion, and
yet what woman
could share her
husband with
another woman
under one roof
and still salvage
her dignity?

Her beauty flowers,
while mine shrivels
and dies, so that his
wandering eye moves
from what he has had
to what he now desires.

I'm afraid
that Heracles
will be called
my husband,
but her lover.

And yet, as
I have said
before, it is
not right for
a practical
woman, such
as myself,
to drown in
her emotions.

I will now reveal
to you how I plan
to deal with this
shameful situation
by administering
a drug that will
kill all the pain.

Long, long ago,
when I was still a girl,
Nessus the centaur
gave me a gift: black
blood in a brass vile,
that had been drained
from a hole in his chest,
just before his death.

He used to ferry
people for a fee
across the river
Evenus, not by

rowing a boat
or sailing a ship,
but by carrying
them in his arms.

One day, the day
on which my father
gave me away,
as I was riding
high over the river
on the centaur's
broad shoulders,
his hungry hands
felt their way up
my legs and groped
me from below.

I shouted for help
and, immediately,
the son of Zeus
released an arrow
from his bow, which
sailed low across
the water and ripped
straight through the
centaur's rib cage,
puncturing his lungs.

He whispered
in my ear
as he wheezed
his last breaths:

"Take the blood
that clots around
this open wound,

where the poison-
tipped arrow has
entered my chest,
spreading the Hydra's
black bile throughout
my broken body,
and you may use
it one day to seduce
the son of Zeus, so
that he will never fall
for another woman."

And so I have kept it,
since his death, locked
away safe, until now.

I have dyed this robe
red and readied it for
Heracles, according
to the instructions
of the dying centaur.

May I never commit
a crime of passion,
for I hate all women
who act irrationally.

But—please—let
this potion work
its magic on my
husband, so he
loses all interest
in Iole and falls
in love with me!

Everything is now in place.

If I have somehow
been blinded by my
jealousy, please speak.

I will abandon the plan.

CHORUS

If you believe the potion
will work, then we believe
your plan will succeed.

DEIANEIRA

I believe it will work,
but cannot be sure, since
I have never tried it.

CHORUS

Since you only
have one chance
to find out, you
will never know
until you try it.

DEIANEIRA

We'll know soon
enough. Look!
Here comes Lichas.
Keep my secret
safe, hold it close,
for nothing can be
shameful if it is
cloaked in silence.

LICHAS *rushes out of the house and*
kneels before DEIANEIRA.

LICHAS

>What are your orders,
>daughter of Oeneus?
>
>We are long
>overdue and
>must return
>immediately.

DEIANEIRA

>Why, Lichas, it's like
>you read my mind!
>
>All of this time,
>while you were
>inside, conversing
>with the captives,
>I was preparing
>this hand-dyed
>robe as a gift
>for my husband.

>>DEIANEIRA *presents the box to* LICHAS.

>Before you give it
>to him, please make
>sure that no one else
>touches it, and do
>not let it be exposed
>to the rays of the sun
>or the raging flames
>of the altar, especially
>when he holds it high
>in the air for all to see,
>including the gods,
>for whom the bulls
>will soon be sacrificed.

This is what I swore
to do if he ever returned
home safely: drape him
in this sacred robe and
show him to the gods,
ready to make sacrifices.

You will bring it to him
as a token of my affection,
which he will immediately
know from the shape of
the seal. Go now and do
not delay another second
or betray your profession
as a messenger, by straying
off-message again, and you
will surely receive thanks
from us both for your service.

LICHAS

If I have ever been faithful
to Hermes, god of messengers,
then I will deliver this casket
to Heracles on your behalf,
just as you have instructed.

DEIANEIRA

Go right away,
and report on
the state of affairs
inside the house!

LICHAS

I will relay
this all to him
right away!

LICHAS *jumps to his feet and runs for the road.*

DEIANEIRA

> And be sure
> to mention
> how you saw
> me welcome
> the girl with
> open arms!

LICHAS (*over his shoulder*)

> Surprising
> us all and
> warming
> our hearts
> with your
> compassion!

LICHAS *disappears from view.*

DEIANEIRA (*to herself*)

> I wonder what
> Heracles will say?

> It might be too
> soon to reveal
> how desperately
> I missed him,
> without knowing
> first if he thought
> of me at all while
> he was away.

DEIANEIRA *goes back inside.*

CHORUS

You who live
near the hot-
sulfur springs
and harbors
east of Trachis
at the foot of
Mount Oeta, and
near the Malian
Sea, and along-
side the coast
most sacred to
Artemis and her
arrows of gold,
where people
from all over
the world are
known to gather,
you will soon
hear the sweet
sound of strings
in the distance,
divinely inspired
by the Muses
in celebration
of Heracles'
triumphant return
after all these
months away
from us, on
the other side
of the ocean,
with no word of
where the winds

had taken him,
as his loyal wife
wasted away in-
side the house,
worried sick
over what might
have happened
to her husband.

But now the war
god Ares, who
stung him into
the madness of
battle, has finally
relented, allowing
him, at long last,
some relief.

If only he would arrive!
If only he would abandon
the altars smoldering with
his sacrifices. If only his
ship would sail here without stopping. If only he
would return with new-
found desire for his wife,
Deianeira, enflamed by
the blood of the centaur!

> DEIANEIRA *appears in the doorway,*
> *wringing her hands, visibly shaken.*

DEIANEIRA

Women, I am afraid
I may have strayed too
far from the path with
my impetuous actions.

CHORUS

What do you
mean, Deianeira?

DEIANEIRA

I do not have
the words
to say it.

I am terrified
by the thought
of what I might
have done.

I tried to do good, but
the record may soon
show that I have done
immeasurable evil.

CHORUS

You don't
mean the gift
you gave
to Heracles?

DEIANEIRA

That is exactly
what I mean.

Never again
will I stand
by in silence,
while someone
I know acts
impulsively, caught up
in the moment,

overwhelmed by
uncontrollable
emotions.

CHORUS

Tell us your
worst fears,
if you're able
to summon
the words.

DEIANEIRA *descends the stairs.*

DEIANEIRA

Something strange
just happened, dear
women, so strange,
you may not believe
it when I tell you.

The liquid in which
I soaked the robe for
Heracles has liquefied
a ball of white wool
that I used to apply
the potion, eroding
the very slab of stone
on which I worked
and then evaporating.

But listen,
there is so
much more
to the story.

I accidentally
overlooked

what the dying
centaur said,
as he choked
back blood,
clutching his
wounded
flank in pain.

I tried to follow
his instructions,
word for word,
as they had been
inscribed in my
mind: never ever
let the fluid see
the light of day
or near an open
flame, until it has
been smeared upon
a piece of fabric!

And this is exactly
what I did only
a few minutes ago,
when I applied it
to the robe behind
closed doors with
a small ball of wool,
recently clipped from
a sheep in our flock,
before folding and
sealing the magical
garment inside a box
made of wood, so
the sun would never

touch it with its rays
until the time was right.

But just now,
as I was leaving
the house, I saw
something that
stopped me in my
tracks and stole
my breath away:
a smoking hole
in the floorboards
where I tossed
the clump of wool
in front of an open
window—as the sun-
light streamed in,
it burned everything
it touched into a fine
gray powder that
floated to the ceiling
and then . . . vanished.

A pool of boiling
blood collected at
my feet and then
turned to mist
before my eyes.

Tell me what to do,
for I have done some-
thing unspeakable.

I somehow imagined
the dying centaur was
on my side, when I
was the reason he died.

But he managed
to get inside my
head and plot
destruction for
the man who had
taken his life.

I see this all
clearly now
that it is too
late to do
anything to
avert the un-
folding disaster
for which
I alone am
responsible.

The arrow
that pierced
the chest of
Nessus kills
everything
in its path.

It even tortured
mighty Chiron,
who is immortal,
and nearly sent
him to his death.

My husband will
never survive
the toxic shock
of the centaur's
black blood when
it enters his body.

His death will be
too hard for me
to witness, and so
it has been decided,
if he must perish,
then I must also
die this day, for
I cannot continue
to live with good
intentions and
face the bitter
consequences of
my evil actions.

CHORUS

This turn of events
is terrifying, but
what makes you so
sure the worst will
happen until you've
seen it take place?

DEIANEIRA

There is no hope
for someone who
has shown herself
to be so misguided.

CHORUS

But when the misguided
make mistakes, they are
more easily forgiven.

DEIANEIRA

You speak like
an innocent by-
stander, but I am
now a criminal.

CHORUS

Instead of speaking
further, it would be
better if you held
your tongue, for here
comes your son
Hyllus, whom you
sent to search for
his father, Heracles.

HYLLUS *appears and shouts at* DEIANEIRA
from the road.

HYLLUS

Oh, Mother!

Either die
or be some-
one else's
mother.

Or, better yet,
go find another
heart to replace
the wicked one
that rattles around
inside your chest.

DEIANEIRA

And what have I done
to deserve your hatred?

HYLLUS *moves toward* DEIANEIRA
with uncontrollable rage.

HYLLUS

You have
murdered
my father,
your husband,
this day!

DEIANEIRA (*cringing with fear*)

Oh, what a horrible
thing to say, my son!

HYLLUS

What I just said
will soon be true;
I speak as a witness,
so I should know.

DEIANEIRA

What are you saying,
my son, and who has
accused me of such
a despicable deed?

HYLLUS

I heard it
from no one,
but saw it with
my own eyes.

DEIANEIRA

Where did you
find him? How
close were you
standing when
you saw him?

HYLLUS

You deserve to hear it;
so I will tell you every-
thing that happened.

After he annihilated
the city of Eurytus,
he carried his spoils
to the altars atop
Mount Cenaeum,
sacred to Zeus,
to make sacrifices.

That is where
I found him
and fell to my
knees, grateful
to still have
a father after
all these months
of worrying
where he was.

And just as he
raised his sword
to slit the throats
of many bulls, his
trusted messenger,
Lichas, arrived

with gifts and
welcome news
from home.

Heracles stretched
out his arms and
slipped on the death-
robe, slaying twelve
bulls without blinking,
the first of hundreds
that were being led
to the slaughter.

At first, his voice
was filled with joy,
as he sang to the gods
in celebration, taking
pleasure in the sacred
fabric, as it draped
ever so elegantly
over his shoulders,
but when the fat began
to fuel the fire, and
the flames blazed
high above our heads,
Heracles started to sweat,
causing the robe to cling
to his skin, as if suddenly
nailed flat by the hand of
an unseen craftsman, and
the first wave of pain shot
through his body, breaking
his bones, eating his flesh,
as the venom raced through
his veins like a hateful snake
constricting him within.

He called out for Lichas,
who was blameless and yet
deeply afraid, and demanded
he explain how he came
to deliver the poison-soaked
robe, and poor Lichas, who
knew nothing, said it was a gift
from you, and you alone, that
he was just following orders.

When Heracles heard these words,
a violent spasm racked his body,
pulverizing his lungs, causing him
to bring up blood. With one hand,
he grabbed Lichas by the ankle and
swung him through the air, bashing
his skull against a boulder, so that
his head exploded on impact,
spraying the air with a pink mist
of brains, blood, and bones.

A collective cry broke through
the silence that followed, as we
witnessed the death of one man
and the annihilation of another,
but not one of us went near him
as he suffered, flailing around on
the ground, screaming and sobbing,
completely consumed by the pain,
as his howls reverberated throughout the surrounding mountains.

Then, in one of the quiet moments,
between the bitter convulsions, as
he cursed your marriage and spoke
spitefully of the disastrous deal he
made with your father, the whites

of his eyes strained to focus through
the low layer of smoke that clung
to his burning flesh, to make out
my face, which by then was stained
with tears from crying in the crowd.

And when he spotted me,
he called out, "Come closer,
Son, and do not turn away
from my suffering, even if it
means you will die at my side.
Hoist up my body and carry it
where no man will be able to
witness what is becoming of
me and, if you have pity for
your father, do not let me die
in this country. Take me away!"

We loaded his broken body
into a ship, according to his
wishes, and sailed straight home,
which was no small struggle, as
he shrieked and shook each time
the poison seized him in its teeth.

This is the whole story,
Mother, of the crime
that you committed
and for which you will
surely be condemned,
as the avenging Furies
hunt you down and,
in the name of Justice,
punish you from above.

I curse you, Mother,
for what you have done,

murdering the noblest
man to ever walk
the earth, whom you
will never see again,
so long as you live!

DEIANEIRA *quietly withdraws inside the house—*
her face, a stone.

CHORUS

Why is she shuffling
away in silence, her
head bowed low, as
if she has something
to hide? Don't you
know your silence
will condemn you?

HYLLUS

Let her go!

And may a strong
gust of wind take
her away from this
place, so I will never
have to see her face
again, for why should
I pretend to respect her
as one respects a mother
when she has stripped
the word of its meaning.

Say goodbye; do not stand
in her way, and wherever
she goes, I hope she enjoys
the same fate as my father.

HYLLUS *runs back to the road and disappears.*

CHORUS

How quickly
the prophecy
has come true.
The son of Zeus
will finally be
relieved of his
labors. These
ancient words
have finally
revealed their
true meaning.

Death shall
be the sweet
relief that he
has long been
awaiting, for
the black blood
of the clever
centaur courses
through his
veins, stinging
his sides, as
the Hydra's
dark poison
eviscerates
his body.

He will never
survive the night,
not when he fixes
his gaze upon
the deadliest of

enemies and
truly begins
to suffer from
the knowledge
that he has been
sentenced to
death by Nessus.

His poor wife
could never have
seen this coming,
when she met
his new bride
and immediately
invited her into
their home, but
she is also partly
to blame for
acting so rashly,
making her
an accomplice
to the crime.

She will never
forgive herself
for what she
has done and,
as she paces
inside, rivers
of tears pour
forth from
her eyes.

Fate reveals
itself as a tragic
calamity dawning
on the horizon.

The dam breaks,
and his cries can
be heard for miles,
as the infection
spreads, desiccating
his godlike flesh
in a matter of seconds,
as no enemy has ever
been able to do before.

We mourn the day
on which he won
his wife, wielding
a black-tipped spear,
while Aphrodite
quietly observed,
showing herself to be
the author of the story.

The NURSE *appears in the doorway, quietly crying.*

CHORUS

Perhaps I am
mistaken, but
I hear weeping
coming from
the house, as
if someone is
covering her
mouth to stifle
cries of grief.

The NURSE *descends the stairs.*

Look how slowly
the nurse is walking
in our direction
with dark circles

under her eyes,
weighed down by
the heavy news
she now carries
on her shoulders.

NURSE

The evil gift,
my children,
that was sent
to lord Heracles
has more in store
for this home.

CHORUS

What is the latest
in this horrible
chain of events?

NURSE

Deianeira
has departed,
setting out on
her final voyage.

CHORUS

She has left us
for the underworld?

NURSE

You heard correctly.

CHORUS

The wretched
woman is dead?

NURSE

Again, you heard correctly.

CHORUS

How did she die?

NURSE

A terrible death.

CHORUS

Tell us now!
How did it happen?

NURSE

She lost the will to live.

CHORUS

But what drove
her to do it,
and how did she
manage to end
her own life,
all by herself,
with a noose
or a sword
or some other
weapon, and
did you happen
to see her take
her last breath,
not that it
matters now?

NURSE

> I saw it. I was
> standing right
> beside her when
> it happened.

CHORUS

> Tell us what you saw!

NURSE

> She cut herself
> with a sharp blade.

CHORUS

> What do you mean?

NURSE

> Exactly as it sounds.

CHORUS

> The child of this
> doomed union
> is the unrelenting
> vengeance of
> the Furies. She
> has delivered
> her own death.

NURSE

> Yes, and you
> would have
> felt sorry for
> her had you
> witnessed it.

CHORUS

> She did this
> with her hand?

NURSE

> It was awful,
> but I will now
> tell you every-
> thing I know,
> so you can hear
> it all and never
> question me
> again about
> what I saw.

> When she dashed into
> the house after speaking
> with her son, she stood
> quietly by the window,
> where she could not be
> seen, and watched him
> saddle his horse before
> riding to find his father.

> She fell to the floor
> and crawled to the altars,
> all the while sobbing
> and choking on tears
> every time her groping
> fingers found some-
> thing from her past.

> She roamed the house
> from room to room,
> breaking down whenever
> she saw the faces of her

servants, weeping more
for herself than for them.

All of a sudden,
I saw her sprint
down the hall
and hurl her body
straight through
the bedroom doors,
where she maniacally
piled blankets high
upon the bed and then
threw herself into
the center, as a steady
stream of tears rained
from her face, and cried:
"Goodbye, marriage
bed. This is the last
time I shall ever
recline upon you,
goodbye." And
with that she pulled
a golden pin from
between her breasts,
causing her robe
to fall to her feet,
exposing her entire
left side, and I ran
and ran as fast as I
could to find her son
and tell him what
she planned to do.

And in the time
it took me to reach
him and return, she

fell upon a double-
edged sword, which
ripped through her
liver and pierced her
twice-broken heart.

As Hyllus surveyed
the damage done by
his mother, he began
to whimper and moan,
for he now understood
that he had cursed her
in anger, hastening her
death, having learned
from the servants about
how she killed her
husband in ignorance,
blindly following the
centaur's instructions.

Then he wept,
as a little boy
weeps when he
misses his mother,
lying along-
side her corpse,
kissing her face,
and cradling
her in his arms,
confessing that
he had wrongfully
accused her of
a crime she did not
willfully commit,
lamenting the loss
of both parents,

mother and father,
in the span of one day.

That is how it is
inside the house.

Anyone who counts
on tomorrow is a fool.

There is no tomorrow
until you've safely
made it through today!

> The NURSE *rushes back into the house.*

CHORUS

I call upon
a gust of wind,
a blast of air,
an upward draft,
to lift me away
from this house
where my heart
will instantly
cease to beat,
frozen with fear,
as soon as my
eyes perceive
the suffering
son of Zeus.

Someone is
said to have
seen him
nearing
the house
just now,
reduced to

inarticulate
sounds,
hounded by
inescapable
pain . . .

Words fall short before suffering.

I cried out
like a king-
fisher,
piercing
the air
with shrill
screaming
when I first
heard the
news of his
diagnosis,
but now I
have been
silenced by
what lies
ahead.

I see them
walking slowly
in the distance,
a group of soldiers
from far away
advancing in
this direction,
carrying his
body carefully,
like medics or
mourners, I can
not be sure,

holding him
closely, as if he
were a relative.

He rides so quietly
on their shoulders.

It is not clear
if he is dead
or just sleeping.

> *A group of* SOLDIERS *carry* HERACLES
> *on their shoulders and place him—*
> *completely still—on the ground.*
> HYLLUS *and an* OLD MAN *follow closely behind.*

HYLLUS

Oh, Father.
My poor father!

What am I
supposed
to do now?

What have
I been born
to suffer?

I am wretched,
wretched!

OLD MAN

Silence, son!

Or you will wake
the untamable pain
with your words.

Your fierce
father still

lives, though
he appears
to be dead.

Bite your lips.
Hold your tongue.

HYLLUS

What did
you just say,
old man?

Did I hear
you say that
he is alive?

OLD MAN

You must not
disturb his
peaceful sleep,
son, or you
will agitate
the savage
affliction
that attacks
him in waves
when he wakes.

HYLLUS

My heart
strains to
speak out,
overloaded
with grief.

HERACLES *begins to stir.*

HERACLES

Oh, Zeus!

Where have
they taken me?

At which men's
feet am I now
splayed out like
a cold corpse,
exhausted
by the endless
waves of pain?

Oh, god.

Here comes the misery.

Here comes the hateful
plague again to ravage
my body, to eat me alive.

Ahhhhhhhhhhhhhhhhh!

OLD MAN

Did I not tell
you to be quiet,
in order to keep
the sick one
from waking?

HYLLUS (*turning away*)

I do not have
the stomach
to bear witness
to this pain.

HERACLES

You altars
of Cenaeum!

I wish I had
never seen
you with my
eyes or made
thanksgiving
sacrifices to
the gods, for
look at what
I received
in return.

This is my thanks.
This is my reward.

A virulent
madness
that shatters
my mind.

A terminal
illness that
shall never
be cured.

For where
is there
a doctor,
other than
Zeus, who
can put this
sickness
to sleep,
who can

sing it into
remission?

It would be
amazing to
meet such
a physician
or even to
hear stories
of his exploits
from afar.

Ahhhhhhhhh!

Let me sleep.
Let me sleep.
Let me close
my wretched
eyelids and
gently slip
away from
this life.

What are
you doing?

The SOLDIERS *hoist him up,*
in order to take him inside.

Do not touch
me. You will
only make it
worse. Enough!

Where are you taking me?
You are killing me. Killing me!

You have awoken the pain
in every fiber of my being.

It has me in its teeth.
Ahhhhhhhhhhhhhhh!

It feeds on me again.
Ahhhhhhhhhhhhhhhh!

> HERACLES *falls to the ground, shaking.*
> *The* SOLDIERS *all scatter in fear.*

Where are you from?
You call yourself Greeks?

You are the most
unrighteous, unjust,
unworthy of men.

I wore myself
down to the bone
for you so-called
Greeks, ridding
your country of
monsters and
exterminating
sea beasts.

Now that I am
the one moaning
on the ground,
clutching my
sides in pain,
will one of you
please come
quickly and visit
me with a sword
or a torch?

AHHHHHHHHHH!

Is there not
one among you
who is willing
to cut off my
head—end

this miserable
existence?

Ahhhhhhhhhhhhh!

The OLD MAN *takes* HYLLUS *aside.*

OLD MAN

Son, this is now
beyond my reach.

I am not strong
enough to save him.

You are the only
one who can
help him through
this final trial.

HYLLUS

I will lay my
hands upon him,
but they will
neither soothe
the pain that
seethes beneath
his skin, nor put
an end to his
endless suffering.

These things are in
the hands of a god.

HERACLES

Ahhhhhhheeeeeeeee!

Where are you, my son?
Come over here and lift me up.

Ahhhhh! Ahhhhh! Ahhhhh!

Oh, god.
Oh, god.
Not again.
Not again.

The savage
contagion
claws through
the walls
of my veins,
bursts through
blood vessels,
and feasts upon
my flesh, inflicting
irreversible damage
and untamable pain.

Ahhhhh, Ahhhhhh, Athena!
It lacerates me from within!

My son. My son.
Show some
compassion for
your father.

Take out your
blameless blade
and make a surgical
incision—right here,
below my collarbone.

Cure the infection
of your mother's
unholy fury com-
busting in my blood.

I wish for her to fall
to her knees and feel
this pain, the very
pain with which she
has destroyed me.

Oh, sweet Hades,
brother of Zeus,
let me sleep
the endless
sleep of sudden
death; relieve
me of my misery.

CHORUS

I shudder at
the sound
of suffering
lord Heracles,
as the illness
ravages his
broken body!

HERACLES

I spent
long years
sweating
and toiling
with coarse
hands over
many hot
labors,
carrying
the weight
of unspeakably

evil memories
on my back.

But never,
in all this time,
have I been
burdened by
anything
devised by
Hera, queen
of the gods,
or King
Eurystheus,
that begins
to approach
the poisonous
web, woven
by my once-
beautiful wife,
Deianeira, and
the avenging
Furies, in which
I now find myself
struggling for life,
waiting for death.

It sticks to my ribs.
It feasts on my flesh.

It invades the lining
of my lungs where it
scrapes against my
chest with every breath.

It guzzles my blood
with unquenchable thirst.

My body is demolished
by an unnatural disaster.

I was never
taken down
by a spear
on the battlefield,
or by the earth-
born army of giants,
or by monsters
or sea beasts,
or Greeks or men
from any other
country, for
that matter.

I was defeated
by a mere female,
a weak woman
without a sword.

My son,
prove your-
self to be my
true-born son.

Curse your mother's
name and drag her out
of the house by her hair
with your hands, then
hand her over to me,
so that I may see you
suffering more at
the sight of my broken
body than at the rightful
defilement of hers.

Come on, my son,
you must find

the strength within
yourself to do this
for your father.

Take pity on me,
for I am worthy
of your pity,
writhing with pain
and weeping
just like a woman,
which no man
can ever say he
witnessed me
do in the past.

I have been stripped
of all my virtue, of
everything that makes
me a man, and reduced
to the state of an animal.

Come closer, Son.

Stand right here
beside me and see
what has become
of your father
in his misfortune.

HYLLUS *moves closer to* HERACLES.

I will expose you
to the truth of my
affliction, pull back
the sheets so you
can see the source
of my misery.

HERACLES *pulls back his robe.*

Open your eyes
wide, all of you!

Look!

Take in
the damage
done by
the disease
to my
tormented
body, gaze
upon a
patient
in pain.

Ahhhhhhhhhhh!
Ahhhhhhhhhhh!
I am wretched!
Ahhhhhhhhhhh!

Here it comes
again, a searing
wave of spasms
moves through
my muscles.

Oh, it burns,
as the vicious
infection shoots
through my veins.

It tortures me
without mercy.

Oh, Hades,
take me now!

Oh, Father
Zeus, bringer

of lightning,
hurl down
your fire-
bolts and
scorch me
from above,
for the disease
is feeding on
me, breaking
out within my
broken body,
replicating
with abandon.

It spreads
into my ex-
tremities:
my hands,
my poor
hands, they
will never
be the same
again; it climbs
my spine
up over my
shoulders,
ripping through
ligaments.

It liquidates
the tissue
within my
once-invincible
arms, with
which I over-
powered

the great lion
of Nemea,
who terrorized
the countryside
unchecked,
afraid of no man.

With these arms
I defeated
the mighty Hydra
of Lerna, and
the savage army
of centaurs,
who in their double
nature, half-stallions–
half-men, trample
their enemies with
cloven hooves
in stampedes of
enormous force,
knowing no laws.

With these arms
I destroyed
the boar of
Erymanthia,
and Cerberus,
the three-headed
hound down in
Hades, the awful
offspring of Echidna,
mother of all monsters.

With these arms
I strangled the serpent
who guarded the golden
apples in the shadows of

Hesperia at the end
of the earth.

I shouldered
the weight of
countless other
labors, facing
down the worst
of adversaries,
but was never
defeated . . .
until now.

All my strength
has been reduced
to rubble, my
nerves have been
shattered, my joints
dislocated, my
muscles shredded.

I am a shell of
my former self.

I am in ruins.

I, who was
the child of
the noblest
of mothers.

I, who was
worshipped
by some
as the son
of Zeus,
taking my
rightful
place in

the sky
among
the stars.

Know this,
above all.

Even if my life
means nothing,
even if I cannot
move another inch,
I will punish
the woman who
did this to me
in spite of my illness.

Bring her to me
so that I may teach
her the meaning
of suffering and
show her how,
in life and in death,
I deal with those
who do me wrong.

CHORUS

Oh, you wretched
Greeks will mourn
the loss of this man
when he is no longer
among the living!

HYLLUS *kneels beside* HERACLES.

HYLLUS

Since in your
silence you have

given me a brief
moment to speak,
please listen closely,
Father, in spite of
your illness, to what
I am about to say.

It is only right for
you to hear me out.

Give yourself over
to the sound of my
voice, without
struggling against
it in anger or
howling with hatred;
unplug your ears
or you will never hear
how your rage has
been displaced and
how you have made
a grave mistake!

HERACLES

Say whatever
you need to say,
then shut your
mouth, my son,
for I am sickened
by the sound of
your voice and,
in my agony,
cannot follow
the logic of
your words!

HYLLUS

I am going to tell
you about my mother
and how she came,
in ignorance,
to make a mistake
and what has now
become of her.

HERACLES

You utterly evil
excuse for a son;
you dare to speak
of the woman
who slaughtered
your father in
earshot of me.

HYLLUS

It would be wrong
to remain silent about
the state she is in.

HERACLES

And what about
the injustice she
has done to me?

HYLLUS

Two wrongs do
not make a right.

Hear what she
has done this day.

HERACLES

> Speak, but do not
> betray yourself
> to be a traitor with
> your words.

HYLLUS

> I will say it.
>
> She is dead.
>
> She died only
> moments ago.

HERACLES *laughs.*

HERACLES

> Your words
> fill me with
> wonder
> and joy!
>
> Who took her life?

HYLLUS

> *She* did.

HERACLES

> Stealing from me
> the satisfaction of
> choking her to death
> with my hands.

HYLLUS

> You would not
> think such things

if you knew what
really happened!

HERACLES

I do not like
the sound of
this, but tell
me what you
think I need
to hear.

HYLLUS

She tried to do
good, but slipped,
and did evil instead.

HERACLES

So you think
it was good
to murder
your father?

Despicable.

HYLLUS

She tried to make
you love her again
by dosing you with
a potion, after laying
eyes on your bride.

HERACLES

And what great physician
gave her this medicine?

HYLLUS

It was Nessus,
the centaur, who,
long, long ago,
taught her how
to reignite your
love with a drug
distilled from
his blood.

HERACLES

Oh.
It is over.

I may as well be dead already.

I see now how my life will end.
The light will fade away forever.

Go gather your brothers
and your sisters; go find my
poor old mother, Alcmene,
who uselessly went to bed
with Zeus, only to give birth
to a son who would one day die.

Bring them all here to my side,
so they can hear my last words.

HYLLUS

I am sorry,
but none of
them are here.

Your mother now
lives at Tiryns along-
side the ocean
with some of your

children; the others
now live in Thebes.

All of us who are here,
Father, will do our best
to assist you, to carry out
your last wishes, and to
make you comfortable.

HERACLES

Well, then listen
to what must
be done, Son.

You are
standing at
a crossroads.

It's time
to show
the world
what you
are made of,
exactly what
kind of man
you have
come to be.

You have long
been called
my son; now
prove yourself,
once and for all,
to be my son.

Long ago,
my father
showed me

the future
and told me
that my life
would never
be ended by
anyone alive,
but that I would
be murdered by
a shade who
lived in Hades.

So Nessus
the Centaur
has killed me
from the grave.

The prophecy was true.
I die at the hand of the dead.

And now I will unlock
the rest of the riddle
that was spoken to me
when I stepped into
the grove of the Selloi,
those high priests at Dodona
who sleep in the mountains
with their feet in the dirt
near the oracular oak
that speaks with many
voices, whispering truth
in the rustling of leaves.

I wrote it all down
so I would not forget.

At this living-
breathing
moment,

when I am
released from
the labors,
long weighing
on my shoulders,
I will finally
be happy.

I see now
what it means.

It means
I will die,
for only
the dead
no longer
labor.

So now that we
know, Son, let's
take action; you
must stay by my
side and never be
pushed away by
my words, no
matter how harsh.

Try not to
provoke my
anger and
work with me
on this last labor,
for the ancient
law is sacred
that requires
a son to obey
his father.

HYLLUS

> Father, it makes
> me uneasy to agree
> with your request, but
> I will do as you ask.

HERACLES

> First, place your
> hand here, right
> against mine.

HYLLUS

> First, tell me
> what compels
> you to make me
> swear an oath.

HERACLES

> Give me your hand quickly,
> and do not defy my orders!

HYLLUS

> Here is my hand.
> I will do as you say.

> HYLLUS *offers up his hand,*
> *which* HERACLES *grips tightly.*

HERACLES

> Swear now
> on the head
> of Zeus who
> gave me life.

HYLLUS

> How can I swear
> until I know what
> I am swearing to do?

HERACLES

> Swear to do
> the deed
> of which
> I speak!

HYLLUS

> With Zeus as my
> witness, I swear.

HERACLES

> Pray to be
> punished if
> you do not
> live up to
> your oath.

HYLLUS

> I will not
> need to be
> punished,
> but I pray
> all the same.

HYLLUS *pulls back his hand.*

HERACLES

> Do you know
> the towering
> mountain of

Oeta, sacred
to Zeus, king
of the gods?

HYLLUS

I know it well,
for I have gone
there many times
to make sacrifices.

HERACLES

Take my body
into your hands,
lift it up with
the help of your
friends, and
carry it there.

Then, chop down
a few of the ancient
oaks firmly rooted
in the earth and
gather branches from
the wild olive groves,
piling high the wood
onto which you
will toss my body.

Then take a flaming
torch made of pine
and set it all ablaze.

Do not let me
see you stifle
cries or choke
on tears of grief.

Do this work
without emotion,
if you are indeed
my son, or I will
lay in wait for you,
even in death, and
visit you with end-
less suffering from
the underworld.

HYLLUS

Father, what
are you saying?

What are you
asking me to do?

HERACLES

What must
be done. Or
be someone
else's son!

HYLLUS

I ask you again,
Father, what are
you asking me
to do—be your
murderer, stained
with the pollution
of your blood,
and hounded by
Furies forever?

HERACLES

> I am asking you
> to be my doctor.
> Heal this affliction!
> Cure my disease!

HYLLUS

> You want me
> to heal your body
> by setting it on fire?

HERACLES

> If you are afraid
> to see this through
> to the end, then
> at least do the rest.

HYLLUS

> I will carry you to Oeta.

HERACLES

> And gather the wood?

HYLLUS

> I will do everything
> that you have asked,
> except light the fire.

HERACLES

> That will be fine.

> Listen, Son, I have one
> last thing to ask of
> you in addition to this.

HYLLUS

Whatever it is,
consider it done.

HERACLES

Do you know
the daughter
of Eurytus?

HYLLUS

Are you
speaking
of Iole?

HERACLES

I am.

Here is what
I want you
to do when
I am dead,
in devotion
to your father
and the oath
that you swore:
take her to be
your bride and let
no other man lay
a hand on this
woman, who
slept next to me
when I was alive.

Do not violate this
small request, when

you have agreed to
grant the larger one,
for in so doing you
will erase all record
of your compassion.

HYLLUS

It is wrong to argue
with the afflicted,
but it is hard to listen to
the twisted logic
of your words.

HERACLES

You speak as if you
are having second
thoughts about every-
thing I have asked.

HYLLUS

Who could say yes
to your request who
knows the actions of
the avenging Furies?

It would be better
to die than to live
with my greatest
of enemies. She
is the reason my
mother is dead
and the source of
all your suffering!

HERACLES

It seems this boy
has no intention
of doing what his
dying father has
asked of him!

Know this, Son.

You will be cursed
by the gods if you
do not give me what
I am rightfully due.

HYLLUS

Your words will soon betray
how sick you really are.

HERACLES

Yes, for you have
enraged the pain,
awakening it again.

HYLLUS

This is impossible.
No matter what
I decide to do,
I will be wrong.

HERACLES

Yes, because you
you think it is right
to disobey a father.

HYLLUS

> If I am loyal
> to you, then
> I am disloyal
> to myself and
> my sense for
> what is right.

> Is this the lesson
> that I am to learn?

HERACLES

> You will learn
> the meaning
> of loyalty
> by granting
> happiness to
> a dying man.

HYLLUS

> Then you order
> me to do this
> with full under-
> standing of what
> you are saying?

HERACLES

> Yes, I call out
> to the gods
> to bear witness
> to my words.

HYLLUS

> Since you have
> shown these deeds

to the gods to be
yours, not mine,
then I will do what
you have asked,
and then no one
will ever be able to
question my loyalty.

HERACLES

In the end,
you have
chosen well,
my son.

Now quickly
do this one last
thing for me.

Take my body
and place it on
top of the pyre,
as I have asked,
before another
wave of pain
comes crashing
down upon me.

Lift me up
right away;
do not wait
another second.

This is the rest
I have long been
awaiting, an end
to my labors and
to mighty Heracles.

HYLLUS

> Nothing will stop
> these things from
> being accomplished,
> since you ordered
> me to carry them
> out on your behalf.

HERACLES

> Do it now!
> Before you
> agitate the
> illness and
> cause me un-
> due suffering.
>
> Oh, unyielding soul!
>
> I will place an iron
> bit between my teeth
> to keep the cries from
> escaping my lips.
>
> Carry out this un-
> pleasant business
> quickly, as if it
> were something
> you wanted to do.

> > HERACLES *places an iron bit in his mouth and*
> > *grimaces, as the* SOLDIERS *hoist his broken*
> > *body on their shoulders, like pallbearers,*
> > *and carry him to the road.*

HYLLUS (*to the* SOLDIERS)

> Hoist him upon your
> shoulders, friends,
> showing compassion
> for what has happened,
> witnessing the brutality
> of the gods toward
> one they called a son.

> No one can say
> what is to come.

> It is heartbreaking
> to helplessly look
> upon this man's
> suffering, and
> shameful for those
> who cause it, but
> hardest of all upon
> the one who suffers
> this affliction.

HYLLUS *and the* SOLDIERS, *carrying* HERACLES,
walk off to the mountain.

CHORUS

> My friends,
> you have seen
> many strange things:
> countless deaths,
> new kinds of torture,
> immeasurable pain,
> and all that you've
> seen here is god.

ACKNOWLEDGMENTS

I would first like to thank my wife, Sarah, and our daughter, Abigail, for filling my life with immeasurable joy, laughter, and love.

I'd also like to express my profound gratitude to Zoë Pagnamenta, Keith Goldsmith, Andrew Miller, William Heyward, Mark Chiusano, Sarah Levitt, and Noam Elcott for their invaluable feedback on this manuscript.

Finally, I would like to acknowledge all of the people who, along the way, have helped me walk this path. A comprehensive list would be pages long, and so, in service of brevity, I will mention only the following individuals, in alphabetical order, without whose friendship, mentoring, and support this book would never have been possible: Marielle Bancou-Segal; Adam, Molly, and Doug Baz; Bronwen Bitetti; Clara, Max, and Leon Botstein; Bil Bowen; Patricia Brennan; Michael Brint; Peter Brook; Ken, Lilly, and Sarah Burns; Megan Byrne; Bill Camp; Amy Cassello; Reg E. Cathey; Marcia Childress; Denyse, Hillary, Lee, and Mark Doerries; Adam Driver; Julie Ehrlich; Jesse Eisenberg; Chuck Engel; Marie-Hélène Estienne; Cliff Faulkner; Margo Figgins; Keith Fowler; Paul Giamatti; Teese and Vicki Gohl; Valley Haggard; Barbara Haskell; Kat Hendrix; Connie Holmes; Doug Hughes; Violaine Huisman; Mary Hull; Shalom Kalnicki; Phyllis Kaufman; Lyuba Konopasek; Taylor Krauss; Eugen Kullmann; Chris Lancaster; Harvey Lichtenstein; George Lombardi; Jill Lundquist; Elizabeth Marvel; Wyatt Mason; Adam Max; Bill McCulloh; Ryan McDermott; Frances McDormand; David McMahon; Charlie Meyer; Bill Mullen; Bill Murray; Bill Nash; Lynn Novick; Brían F. O'Byrne; Fifi Oscard; Jim Ottaway; Drew Patrick; Benita Polonio; Dave Rath; Royal Rhodes; Randy Riggs; Don Rogan; Sally Rogan; Jamie Romm; Jon, Laura, and Mary Rothenberg; Susan Rutter; David Sampliner; Jonathan Shay; Nelson and Virginia Smith; David Strathairn; Tyler Studds; Michael Stuhlbarg; Loree Sutton; Feli Thorne; Joanne Tucker; Elisabeth Turnauer-Derow; Tom Turgeon; Geoffrey C. Ward; Laura Weber; Robert Weimann; Irene Zedlacher; and Andrew Zolli.